MW01077420

Footprints

Secret Lives at Bletchley Park

Philomena Liggins

HIDDEN TALENTS
PUBLISHING

Philomena Liggins, Hidden Talents Publishing
3a South House, The Bond Estate, Bond Avenue
Bletchley, Milton Keynes MK1 1SW
www.hiddentalents-uk.com

This novel is based on historical fact and every effort has been made to present correct information. The war-time story is told through the lives of fictional characters and no similarities are intended or implied. The names of code-breakers and other individuals mentioned in the book are included to confirm the work they carried out. Any interaction between characters is fictional in order to tell the story.

Footprints/Philomena Liggins/1st Edition
ISBN-13: 978-1500879877

DEDICATION

"In the face of adversity and within the confines of that most secret place, there was a freedom which crossed the great divides of British society. This place was, if nothing else, a melting pot of diverse talents and personalities, the like of which would never be seen again".

Between 1939 and 1945 it is understood that up to 10,000 people worked at Bletchley Park and its outstations. Drawn from all walks of life and with varying skills, those people came together with one single aim.

It is to each and every one of them, that this book is dedicated.

Philomena Liggins
September 2013

TESTIMONIALS

Easy to read story, full of facts. Well worth buying.

I bought this after a fascinating day out at Bletchley Park and I wanted to know more. This book has helped me to take in the vast amount of information available, a bit like being on the very interesting tour all over again. It is deceptively easy to read this charming story that cleverly weaves the facts into the fictional story of two young girls recruited to work at Bletchley.

What a great little novel, everyone should read it!

This story intrigues you from the beginning to the end, it has some lovely twists in it and leaves you wanting more, I couldn't put it down!

Loved it and will read it again

This story about the lives of those at Bletchley Park was totally absorbing. The historical accuracy of events as the story unfolded made a very moving story even more credible. The first couple of chapters, setting the scene seemed to move quite slowly but then set off at a great pace. I feel it gives insight as to the grave situation of World War 11 and how many brave people from all walks of life played a vital role.

A charming tale of the lives of two operators at wartime Bletchley Park.

The characters are (probably) imaginary but are skillfully woven into a detailed, factual background by an author who clearly knows her stuff

Contents

Sunrise

SHE WOKE WITH THE QUICK CHILL AS HE LEFT THE BED. The room was in darkness save for a shaft of light coming in from the landing. Downstairs she heard the comforting early morning banter between man and dog, followed by the welcome sound of the kettle being fuelled for the first cup of tea of the day. She lay there for a while adjusting her eyes to the semi-darkness. Any moment now their little dog would come bounding up the stairs, jump on the bed and settle down beside her. As if on cue, the dog nosed open the bedroom door, letting in more light together with the measured tones of the BBC newsreader drifting up from the kitchen below. She strained her ears to listen to the muted report of the previous day's bombings, and gently stroking the little dog, wondered when this war would ever end.

Jim came into the room with her early morning cup of tea, set it down on the bedside table and switched on the light. It was 7 o'clock and he was dressed and ready to leave for his monthly meeting in London. The previous evening he had booked a taxi to take him the short journey to Bletchley Railway Station in order to catch the morning train. Bidding his wife a fond farewell, he kissed her on the forehead and went down the stairs just as his taxi arrived.

In the quiet of the house Susan sat up in bed, sipped her tea and began to prepare herself for the day. As the cold light of the December morning filled the room she tugged herself from the comfort of the warm bed and carefully selecting her clothes, she laid them out neatly before going into the bathroom. When she had finished, she wrapped herself in her warm dressing gown and went downstairs; their little dog following attentively behind her.

Sitting at the kitchen table she opened her diary to confirm her schedule and noted that she was not due on the Park until 10 o'clock. Excellent, that meant she had plenty of time to read her mail and scan through the news before getting ready for work. Checking the kettle for water she placed it on the gas ring and looked out through the kitchen window across the garden beyond, and lost herself in thought.

Outside the deep frost lay like a dusting of snow on the ground revealing tiny paw prints, evidence of the dog's early morning patrol of his territory. The dark trees formed a sharp contrast against the clear blue sky, and Susan watched as a hungry squirrel scuttled through the branches sending flurries of frost silently to the ground. Throughout the garden the network of gossamer threads glistened in the sunlight. Susan loved this time of year, it was still, quiet and ever so slightly eerie and shivering involuntarily, she pulled her dressing gown closer around her body.

It was then that the shrill sound of the boiling kettle brought her attention sharply back to the kitchen. Instinctively she warmed the tea pot, lifted the lid from the caddy and dropped a spoon of tea into the pot before adding the boiling water. Leaving the tea to brew, she toasted a slice of bread and sat back at the table. The dog curled up on the floor beside her and rested his head on her slipper.

Twenty minutes later, having finished her toast and Marmite, Susan eased her foot from beneath the dog's head and went back upstairs to get dressed. Before breakfast she had selected the neat woollen maroon and cream checked two-piece costume and placed it on the bed next to her cashmere jumper, silk slip and stockings. Dress code on the Park was smart casual and Susan maintained a modest range of outfits strictly for that purpose. Picking up the stockings she sat on the stool by the dressing table, turned her diamond engagement ring into the palm of her hand and being careful not to snag them, slowly rolled each stocking on to her legs. Fully fashioned stockings were hard to come by these days, and these were her only pair.

With her stockings safely secured Susan put on her slip, jumper and skirt before returning to the dressing table. Picking up the tail comb she styled her hair and, though she found it difficult to achieve the fashionable hair roll of the time, she knew her hat would cover a multitude of sins. With her hair in place she opened her make-up case and leaning towards the mirror, thought a spot of eye shadow, lipstick and powder would suffice.

Finally, lifting the lid of the jewellery box she took out her mother's gold watch. It was an excellent time-piece and after checking the time with the bedroom clock, she clasped it around her wrist. Reaching back into the box she chose a pair of pearl ear rings and clipped them in place, smiling at her reflection in the mirror as she did so. However, the face that smiled back was not Susan's, it was her mother's. She sat for a while, as she did on these occasions, then with a wink of the eye and a loving smile she averted her gaze, closed the jewellery box and knew it was going to be an interesting day.

Slipping her shoes on, she turned her legs to check her seams. Pulling on her jacket she went over to the wardrobe and selecting the camel coat, folded it neatly over her arm. Collecting her hat and fur from their stand, she picked up her handbag and gloves and hurried out of the bedroom.

Downstairs the dog had taken up sentry duty snoozing on the chaise in the hall below. On hearing the sound of her footsteps he slowly opened his eyes and looked up. He knew her every move. She would put her handbag, hat and gloves on the table and go into the kitchen to lock the back door. Returning to the hall she would make a fuss of him, pick up her hat and handbag, check the time on the hall clock with her wrist watch, and leave the house. As Susan closed the door behind her the little dog watched and waited for her imminent return.

Jim's footprints were still visible on the path and walking gingerly over the frosty ground Susan made her way to the car. Unlocking the door she placed her hat, coat and fur neatly in the back and slipped into the driver's seat. Putting her handbag on the passenger's seat next to her, she realised that she had forgotten her gloves. Quickly returning to the house she retrieved the gloves from the hall table, repeated her goodbye to the little dog and firmly closed the door behind her.

The dog waited until he heard the sound of the car's engine and listened as it pulled away into the distance. Satisfied his mistress had left, he settled down to a peaceful slumber.

Susan had chosen to take the back lanes to the Park, out along the Newport Road, past the Simpson School and School House; on through Simpson village; up over the hump backed bridge which crossed the Grand Junction Canal and into Fenny Stratford. This route was always quiet and as long as she was not stopped by the Bletchley to Bedford train at the Fenny Station's level crossing, she should be at Bletchley Park in less than fifteen minutes.

On the dot of nine forty-five, Susan drove up to the entrance and stopped at the gate as Clarence came out to greet her. Though he knew all the personnel and vehicles on the Park, a recent security alert had prompted that passes must be checked. Susan did not mind as these days increased security had become part of daily life. Checking both her vehicle and her pass, Clarence opened the gate and waved her through.

Footprints

Taking a sharp right between the stark brick buildings Susan drove up towards the Mansion and parked in her usual space by the tennis courts. It was certainly chilly, and getting out of the car she quickly put on her coat, fur wrap and hat. Picking up her handbag and gloves from the passenger seat she checked her hat in the rear window and pulling on her gloves, hurried towards the front of the Mansion.

Bletchley Park

The Victorian Mansion

THE NINETEENTH CENTURY MANSION had been set in sixty acres of gardens and woodland and was the epitome of a Victorian English country house, boasting a range of architectural and decorative styles, including Dutch, Italian, Old English, Medieval and Tudor; the latter being favoured by the wealthy Victorian society of the time. The original smaller gentleman's house had been built in 1878 by architect and businessman Samuel Lipscombe Seckham. However, within five years Seckham had sold the estate to wealthy financier Herbert Samuel Leon who, together with his wife Fanny, would make their mark on the family country home, creating an enigma of a building, the image of which would become synonymous with the code-breakers of the Second World War.

Susan walked across the tennis courts and noticed that the Park was strangely quiet. Only the tell tale footprints that criss-crossed the frosty ground between the Mansion and the huts provided any evidence of life.

Shivering from the cold Susan welcomed the warmth of the house as she entered the large wood panelled Entrance Hall and made her way over to the desk. Taking off her gloves she picked up the pen, signed her name in the log book and glancing over her shoulder at the clock, registered her arrival as 9:50. Placing the pen back into its holder she stood for a moment and listened for the customary sound of muffled voices coming from the Library, Drawing Room or Dining Room as Margaret and Joyce prepared the house for the day. There was nothing. Just like the grounds, the Mansion seemed empty and still.

Returning her attention back to the desk she saw the colour-coded folders neatly labelled and organised; a sure sign that both ladies were most definitely on site. Sliding the pink folder from the pile Susan opened it to check her schedule. Her group of fifty visitors were due to arrive at 10:30 for coffee, followed by a tour of the grounds at 11 o'clock, lunch at 12:30 and tea at 3:30 before departing at 4 o'clock when the Park closed for the day. Apart from the usual visitor badges and schedule in the folder, there was a hand written note from Margaret advising Susan of an envelope that had been left in her pigeon hole in the Guides' room.

Susan had been a Volunteer Tour Guide at Bletchley Park since 2007 and like many others who worked there she had been drawn to this quirky Victorian house and its extra-ordinary war-time past. However, no matter how quirky or mysterious, there were some parts of the house that Susan avoided and would prefer remained both secret, and most firmly in the past. The back service staircase and the Guides' room were just two of those places. Unfortunately, the only way to access the Guides' room was by those back stairs.

Deciding to collect her envelope, Susan took the shortest route and walked through the ornate Entrance Hall, with its Italian marble columned arches and on into the baronial Billiard Room. Turning right she opened a door which took her from the opulence of Victorian decadence straight into the austerity of the Servants' Hall and the narrow back staircase leading to the rear first floor landing.

During the Leon times, the bedrooms on that landing were set aside for the personal servants of visiting house guests. Over the years there had been many changes and the rooms were now used as offices and storage with the Guides' room at the dead end of the windowless passage. Regardless of ghost stories and gossip associated with the backdrop of any Victorian Mansion, Susan had always felt uncomfortable in that part of the house. Each time she climbed those stairs and made her way along that dark passage she wondered what it was like to have been a visiting lady's maid in a strange house and who, if anyone, had met their death at the foot of those stairs.

On reaching the Guides' room Susan quickly keyed in the code, opened the door and securing it with her left foot stretched across the narrow room. Retrieving the envelope from her pigeon hole she turned on her heel, letting the door close firmly behind her and hurried back towards the top of the staircase. Taking a firm grip of the banister and with the comforting sound of her own regular footfall on the bare wood, she stepped carefully and purposefully down the very steep, narrow flight of stairs.

Safely back on the ground floor Susan returned to the Servants' Hall and was greeted by the welcome hubbub of voices in the distance and checked her wrist watch just as the bells of near-by St Mary's Church struck 10 o'clock. The first of the day's coach parties had arrived bringing the house back to life.

With the silence broken, Susan replaced fantasy with reality and stepped out of the quiet of the Victorian Servants' Hall into the bustle of the twenty-first century. This place was, if nothing else, a place of contrasts and contradictions; a true enigma in itself.

Susan entered the Billiard Room and saw Joyce, folder in hand, making sure that all her charges were suitably identified with their pink visitor's badges before ushering them into the Ballroom for their hurriedly arranged morning coffee. It was obviously Susan's group that had arrived early and putting the letter she had retrieved from her pigeon hole firmly in her handbag, she walked back through to the Entrance Hall where Margaret was already making adjustments to the day's schedule.

Looking up from the desk Margaret smiled, "Good morning Susan, your group has just arrived and Joyce is organising their coffee. There are only forty-eight, as the veteran and her daughter couldn't come."

It was always a privilege to welcome a veteran back to the Park. Since the last of the Second World War code-breakers had left in 1945, some of them had chosen never to return, some continued to make the annual trip to the Enigma Reunion, whilst others came back just for one last time. Though Susan was disappointed that she wouldn't be meeting a veteran today, she completely understood, most especially with this inclement weather.

Taking that weather into consideration Susan checked with Margaret to see if she could take her group out earlier and make full use of Hut 11 where they would be able to sit down out of the chill wind. Whilst Joyce looked after their guests in the Ballroom, Margaret and Susan amended the schedule and agreed the new timings. Even in the winter months the Park still attracted many visitors and moving groups seamlessly around the grounds required military precision.

With her amended schedule, Susan checked her hat, pulled the fur wrap closer around her shoulders and walked into the Ballroom to greet their visitors and take them back in time to the 1940s war-time workings of Bletchley Park.

{ 3 }

A Secret Site

The Government Code & Cypher School

UCKED AWAY IN THE RELATIVE SAFETY OF
THE BUCKINGHAMSHIRE COUNTRYSIDE,
Bletchley Park had been selected as the
secret war-time base for the Government Code &
Cypher School. After the death of the widow Fanny
Lady Leon in January 1937, the Bletchley Park estate
had been auctioned off in separate lots and by 1938,
for all intent and purpose, the Mansion and some of the
grounds had become the property of Admiral Hugh
Sinclair. Sinclair was head of the British Secret

Intelligence Service, and this Victorian pile presented with excellent credentials that he could not ignore.

Situated forty-five miles north of London, the old Leon estate was skirted by Watling Street, a 260 mile stretch of Roman road which straddled the country, linking Marble Arch in London to Admiralty Arch at Holyhead in Wales. On the edge of the estate, just a short walk from the Mansion, was Bletchley Railway Station and its busy junction, with the London Midland and Scottish Railway Company providing trains to major towns and cities including Bedford, Cambridge, Glasgow, London, Manchester and Oxford. Together with the excellent road and rail links this Buckinghamshire backwater also presented Sinclair with access to the state of the art tele-communications with the General Post Office repeater station at nearby Fenny Stratford, boosting the signals along the Watling Street underground cables. This place was, if nothing else, well located to accommodate the communication needs of the secret organisation assigned to break the enemy codes and ciphers.

One such cipher was the Enigma cipher. Enigma is another word for puzzle and was the name given to a machine that quite simply, turned one letter into another letter. That, however, was where the simplicity stopped, and the complexity began. Due to its internal wiring and component settings, only those with the knowledge of the settings could turn text into gobble-de-gook, and vice-versa. The Enigma machine was therefore, a vehicle through which a message could be translated from plain language into a string of jumbled letters. This string of mixed-up letters was then transmitted by radio using Morse code. Anyone listening in over the airways could write down the Morse code, but remain ignorant of the content of that message. Only the sender and the recipient, using the stipulated Enigma machine settings, could both encipher and decipher that message and read it.

This portable cipher machine, which looked a bit like a typewriter in a wooden box, was used, amongst others, by the German Navy, Army, Air Force, Intelligence and Transport services. Each one of those sections or networks, with their own cache of Enigma machines and settings were able to encipher thousands of messages a day for wireless transmission across the airways. Meanwhile in wireless listening stations around Britain those radio messages were being intercepted; but without knowledge of the Enigma machines' settings, each message remained locked behind a jumble of meaningless letters.

As head of Britain's Secret Intelligence Service, one of Sinclair's tasks was to consolidate the brains of Oxford, Cambridge and Manchester Universities in order to find those Enigma settings, un-lock the messages and present the contents to the appropriate services. Drawing on the skills of the original pool of the First World War code-breakers from the Admiralty's Room 40 and the Military's MI1B, together with engineers, linguists, mathematicians, scientists, chess players, crossword puzzle enthusiasts, typists, clerks, businessmen and thespians; the members of the Government Code & Cypher School gathered at Bletchley Park in September 1939 to take up the cipher challenge.

At the height of the Second World War nearly 10,000 people worked at Bletchley Park and it's out stations. They all signed the Official Secrets Act of 1911 and 1920, requiring them to adhere to complete secrecy about the place they worked, and the work they did. Out of that 10,000, it is believed that 6,000 of them were women civilians and military personnel, including members of the Women's Royal Naval Service, affectionately known as the Wrens.

Many of those Wrens worked in the hastily erected wooden huts and reinforced brick buildings which erupted within the walls of Bletchley Park's secret garden. Being in the Royal Navy, the Wrens followed naval protocol, procedures and terminology and those drafted to work at Bletchley Park served on the land locked HMS Pembroke V, from where they would play their part in many battles.

In the face of adversity and within the confines of that most secret place there was a freedom which crossed the great divides of British society. This place was, if nothing else, a melting pot of diverse talents and personalities the like of which would never be seen again.

{ 4 }

Bletchley Park
at War

A Walk in the Park

BACK IN THE MANSION, having introduced her group to Bletchley Park, Susan prepared them for a walk in the grounds and with impeccable timing Joyce opened the double doors of the Ballroom just as Susan was about to lead her group out. Coming over to Susan, Joyce slipped the kid gloves into her coat pocket and whispered, "You left these on the desk. You will need them. It is cold out there."

Susan whispered a grateful, "Thank you," and pulling on her gloves she took the group out of the warmth of the Mansion into the biting chill of the December day.

Joyce was right. It was bitterly cold and within moments of hitting the winter air Susan's nose registered red on the chill factor scale of pink to bright red, and she chose to keep her group gently on the move whilst showing them the war-time landmarks of Bletchley Park.

From the vantage point at the rear of the Mansion they were shown one of the Park's guarded entrances through which the despatch riders came carrying their bags of intercepted messages. From that same vantage point the group could see the Leon's water tower used by MI6 in the early years as a radio station to maintain contact with their agents working as Passport Control Officers in selected British Embassies across Europe.

In the Stable Yard Susan told the group about the pigeon loft, home to MI6 pigeons dropped behind enemy lines in order to fly back home carrying agents' messages. They were shown Cottage 3 where the famous Room 40 code-breaker Dilly Knox worked with his group of loyal young ladies, and before moving on the group were able to take photographs of the Polish Memorial, the tribute to the Polish code-breakers of the Second World War.

Footprints

On leaving the relative shelter of the Stable Yard a sharp blast of wind came across the open tennis courts, sending a flurry of frost from the trees down over the group below and thinking on her icy cold feet Susan decided to take her group directly into the shelter of Hut 11.

Hut 11 was a single story brick building often referred to as the Bombe Room, taking its name from the six large Letchworth or Turing Bombe machines housed there during the early years of the Second World War. As Susan approached the building's double doors she turned the Bakelite handle and pushed one of the doors open; securing it on the hook on the wall. Like all the other war-time buildings it was stark and cold, built fit for purpose with its thick reinforced brick walls, concrete floor and four small windows down either side, providing the only source of daylight. It is no wonder that the Wrens working in there during the war called it "the hell hole". In that place, twelve Wrens worked on each of the three, eight hour watches, around the twenty-four hour clock. Their single aim was to reduce the time taken to identify the machines' settings of those intercepted Enigma messages.

As the members of Susan's group filed into the building they each murmured grateful sighs of appreciation to be out of the chill wind and eagerly took their places on the chairs provided. Glancing at the clock, strategically placed so that Guides did not overstay their slot, Susan checked the time with her watch and took up her post by the prop Bombe machine, a remnant from the film *Enigma*.

This was the place where Susan introduced the visitors to the stark reality of Bletchley Park in those early years bringing alive the working conditions, the pressures, frustrations and the sadness even in times of triumph. Using a German Naval Enigma message as an example, Susan followed its journey from a radio intercept station somewhere in England, to the saddle bag of the despatch bike; from the despatch bike onto the desk of a code-breaker in Hut 8 and then to a Bombe machine in Hut 11. If the Enigma machine settings were found, the information gleaned from the message would be sent to Hut 8's Naval Decrypt Section and onwards to Naval Intelligence in Hut 4, then out into the theatre of war.

Working with a jumble of letters that was an enemy message, Alan Turing's team in Hut 8 used their intelligence to calculate a link which they believed could provide the key to break into that message. In order to test their theory they sent their computation, called a Menu, through to the Wrens in Hut 11 who set up a Bombe machine accordingly. The machine was switched on, and with a continuous, repetitive, mechanical clatter it rolled into action to begin the process of elimination. When the machine stopped, it hopefully provided the code-breakers with a major part of the settings of that particular message. If successful and the cipher was broken, all other messages on the same network using the same Enigma settings could also be read for the remainder of the twenty-four hour period, or until those settings were changed .

However, as Susan explained, it was not all plain sailing. The work was quite literally a battle against time. It was particularly stressful for those working in Hut 8 in the early years. After an initial break-through in 1941, Alan Turing and his team had been locked out of German Naval Enigma for the nine months between February and November of 1942. The devastation caused by the German U-boats on allied shipping took its toll, and Hut 8 was under constant pressure to get results.

With an Enigma story told, Susan brought her group back from the carnage of the Atlantic Ocean to a stunned silence which was now Hut 11 some seventy years later. Letting her group acclimatise to the present day she waited a while before glancing up at the clock and inviting them to follow her back to the Mansion for their lunch.

As Susan took her visitors out of the hut and across the tennis courts she noticed another group preparing to move onwards from outside Hut 6. Their Guide lifted his hand and waved a sign of appreciation as he too ushered his party into the comparative shelter of "the hell hole". Even in the twenty-first century, teamwork and timing was of the essence.

Back in the Mansion Joyce and Margaret welcomed their guests, guiding them towards the Ballroom and their hot lunch. Due to the worsening weather conditions the coach driver had asked if they could leave Bletchley slightly earlier and as Joyce attended to the group, Margaret and Susan once again rearranged the afternoon schedule.

So, as the winter sun slipped in the afternoon sky marking the shortest day of the year, the coach pulled away from the front of the Mansion slightly earlier than originally planned, and Joyce and Susan waved their visitors goodbye.

Returning to the warmth of the building the two women went over to the desk where Margaret was catching up with the paperwork. It had been a good day, all the coaches were safely on their way home, the other Guides had signed out and Susan prepared to do the same. Picking up the pen she automatically glanced over her shoulder to check the time on the hall clock and logged it as 3:40. Returning the pen to its holder, she hooked her handbag over her shoulder and reaching deep into her coat pockets for her gloves let out a huge sigh. Margaret and Joyce both looked up from the desk, and with a knowing glance said, "Gloves?"

Casting her eyes up to the heavens and pulling a face of sheer frustration, indicating that she had done it yet again, Susan simply nodded and replied, "Yes."

They all laughed and the three women verbally retraced Susan's footsteps before she realised that she had left her gloves on the table by the Bombe in Hut 11. Exchanging season's greetings with Margaret and Joyce, Susan left the Mansion and made her way once again across the tennis courts and back to "the hell hole".

The door of Hut 11 was closed and the Bakelite handle was cold to the touch as Susan turned it to let herself in. On entering the building she adjusted her eyes to the semi darkness and was reaching for the light switch when she let out a sudden gasp. Sitting in one of the chairs was an elderly lady. Hearing Susan enter the room the lady turned around and said, "I am so sorry my dear. I did not mean to startle you. I am just waiting for my friend. She won't be long."

Gathering her composure and telling her heart to return from her throat to its rightful place in her chest cavity, all sorts of thoughts ran through Susan's mind. What was this dear lady doing here at this time of day? Had she been forgotten? Had they miscounted the coach parties? Where was her friend?

"Oh, that's all right," Susan squeaked, in a voice she did not recognise as her own, "I was just a little shocked to see you here. Would you like to come back with me to the Mansion? It's warmer in there and we can radio to find your friend?"

The lady smiled reassuringly, "No thank you. I am quite comfortable here. I am not cold and my friend knows where I am."

The lady motioned Susan to a chair and asked, "Would you sit with me a while?"

Glancing at the clock Susan noticed it was 3:50pm and Tony would be on his rounds locking up. Susan knew that he would come inside to check the building first and he could call on his radio to arrange to take the lady to the comfort of the Mansion and find her friend.

Sitting down opposite the lady Susan introduced herself.

"My name is Susan. I am a Tour Guide."

"Yes my dear, I know who you are," replied the lady, "I heard your talk earlier."

Susan's new found composure turned to panic as the thought flashed through her mind that one of her group had indeed been left behind. She had not long since waved her party off and was sure she had counted them all back on the coach. Anyway Joyce would never have let the coach leave without double checking. Susan cast a furtive glance to see if she could see a pink day visitor's badge on the lady's coat.

As if reading Susan's mind the lady smiled reassuringly, "Do not worry my dear. No one has left me behind," and then added, with what Susan thought was a twinkle in her eye, "I do not need a badge."

The realisation set in as Susan asked the lady if she had been to the Park before.

"Oh yes my dear, many, many times. I used to work here," she replied.

Of course, thought Susan, this lady is a veteran and has the Freedom of the Park, so she would not need a day badge. Then, speaking out loud she continued, "Forgive me. I'm so sorry, I didn't realise. You are one of our veterans."

The lady smiled once again and said, "Well if that is what you call us, then yes that is what I am."

"Are you sure you wouldn't prefer to wait for your friend in the Mansion?" Susan asked once again,

"Tony will be here shortly to lock this building for the night and we can all walk back together."

"Oh do not worry. We will be gone before he comes. My friend will not be long. We had arranged to meet here. She worked here too."

Susan's eyes widened as another thought flashed through her mind. Do we have two veterans on site?

"You both worked here?" Susan questioned.

"Yes, we both came on the same day in the summer of 1942."

As the lady spoke Susan felt herself being transported back in time, becoming a most privileged observer of the secret lives of two war-time friends and the part they played in the Battle of the Atlantic

.

The Journey

August 1942

THE STEAM TRAIN SLOWLY PULLED OUT OF EUSTON STATION IN LONDON and began its long journey north. In one of the carriages a young lady wearing her new blue naval uniform sat by the window. Like the rest of the train, the carriage was full. Sitting opposite her was a studious young man scribbling notes on a piece of paper. Next to him was an older man with his eyes closed in contemplation, sucking on an unlit pipe. By the carriage door a mother cradled a sleeping baby, whilst her young son fidgeted beside her. Wedged between his mother and the side of the carriage the boy pulled up his knee length socks in an attempt to shield his bare legs from the rough horse hair filled seats.

The man sitting opposite them put down his newspaper, reached into his briefcase and pulled out a copy of the Dandy and handed it to the boy. The boy looked up at his mother who nodded approval and smiled. Politely accepting the comic the child immediately lost himself in the adventures of Desperate Dan. Glancing at his wrist watch the man returned his attention to his newspaper and continued the Telegraph crossword.

Next to the man with the crossword was a smartly dressed officious looking gentleman holding tightly onto a buff coloured attaché case. Whilst next to him, was a rather scruffy young man with unkempt hair. Outside in the corridor a group of soldiers going home on leave sat on their kit bags, smoking Woodbine cigarettes and showing each other photographs of girl friends, wives and children.

As the train moved on leaving London behind, the grey houses, factories and bombed out shells of buildings were replaced by a patchwork of colourful fields dotted with farm houses, cottages and barns. Farmers on horse drawn carts worked in their fields making the most of the long summer days. Children sat on track side fences eagerly waving as the train went by; and the occasional motor car waited at the railway level crossings. Everywhere across England there were similar pockets of countryside which unlike the major towns and cities, including Birmingham, Bristol, Coventry, Hull, Liverpool, London, Manchester and Newcastle, had escaped the bombing and seemed deceptively untouched by war.

Looking out over this illusion of peace the young lady reflected on the past few months. She had returned from Canada with her mother and on arriving back in England she had told her parents that she wanted to join the Wrens to do her bit for her country. Her father had tried to dissuade her, saying that he could secure her a good job at the Foreign Office where they were always on the lookout for girls like her with language and secretarial skills. She had argued bitterly saying that she did not want to be stuck in an office on a typewriter or sit translating German all day. With her mind made up, her mother had taken her father to one side and suggested that he make full use of his network of friends to secure their daughter a suitable place.

All was agreed and she volunteered to join the Women's Royal Naval Service. After passing the strict medical and the initial training she had been called to a selection board, signed the Official Secrets Act and within weeks was sitting on a train going to a place that, until two days earlier, she had never heard of.

She had, however, found it somewhat curious that when she had telephoned her father to tell him she had been drafted to a place in the country, he did not seem at all surprised.

In the next compartment another young Wren sat looking out over the countryside and thinking about the last few months. Her cousin Peter had come home on leave before being assigned to the merchant ship the M.V. Athelsultan sailing out of Liverpool, and the two cousins had sat in their childhood den talking about the war. Peter's Dad had been gassed at Ypres in 1917 and had returned from France a broken man. Though he had come back home to his village in County Durham and married his childhood sweetheart, he had died when Peter was a small child and Peter's Mam had never got over what the war had done to her husband.

With the outbreak of war in 1939 Peter had promised his Mam that he would not follow his Dad into the Durham Light Infantry; instead he volunteered to join the Navy. So it was on a winter's evening in 1942 as the two cousins said their goodbyes, she had known, that for some strange reason she too would join the Navy.

When she told her parents what she intended to do, her Mam and Dad thought that she would be better joining the Auxiliary Territorial Service (ATS) as a driver. She was considered to be a bit of a tomboy and had always liked tinkering about with machines and cars and had helped Mr Heppell in his garage when his mechanics had been called up to war. In return Mr Heppell had taught her to drive and she had even driven Mr Blenkinsop's charabancs around the yard when they were in the garage for repair. Though the driving test had been suspended on the outbreak of war, Mr Heppell said that she was a good driver and would easily pass any driving test, pointing out that the First Aid Nursing Yeomanry (FANY) and the ATS had their own driving test, which would put her in good stead for after the war.

Both her Grandparents had agreed and her Ma had thought she would be best going up to Alnwick as Great Aunt Edith had said that the Duchess of Northumberland had formed a FANY Corp up at the castle and needed girls to drive the ambulances. Her Da had said that her late Uncle Jack had nothing but praise for those ladies of the FANY who went to war and put their lives in danger to administer first aid; comforting the dying and ferrying the wounded from the front line back to the field hospitals. However, no matter what her Grandparents had said, she thought the ladies of the FANY Corps were a bit above her station and anyway, she hated the sight of blood. With regards to driving, she most certainly did not want to drive a charabanc, nor a car, let alone an ambulance; nor did she want to work with smelly, dirty, noisy oily machines. So with everyone's blessing she volunteered for the fresh sea air and following in her Cousin Peter's footsteps; she joined the Navy.

Like the young Wren in the train compartment next to hers, she too had passed the strict medical, been before a selection board, signed the Official Secrets Act and within days was on her way to a place she had never heard of. The previous evening she had sat down and written her Mam a letter telling her she was moving to the country but that she could not say where, though she would write again soon with her billet address.

Approaching the station the train slowed down and the men in the next compartment started to put their papers away. The boy offered the comic back to the man opposite him, who gestured that he could keep it. The child's face lit up as he thanked the man and held the comic close to his chest.

Making his way along the train's corridors the Guard climbed over men and kit bags shouting, "Bletch-ley, Bletch-ley,"

Then, opening the door of the compartment he looked straight at the young lady in her blue uniform and said, "Come on mi lady, time to get off."

The Wren looked back at him and wondered how he knew where she was getting off the train, and as if responding to an order she immediately stood up and reached for her kit bag neatly stowed on the luggage rack above her head. As she did so the train jerked to a sudden halt, and losing her balance she fell straight into the lap of the studious young man opposite her. Feeling her face burn with embarrassment she apologised profusely and got to her feet, straightening her skirt and trying desperately to rescue her pride. The studious young man did not say a word; he just smiled. The scruffy young man who had been sitting next to her reached up and lifted her bag down from the luggage rack, placed it on her seat and whispered in her ear, "I'll probably see you up there."

She looked back at him with a puzzled expression, wondering how on earth he thought that he could possibly know where she was going.

Apart from the soldiers and the young mother with her two children, it seemed as if the whole train had poured the rest of its passengers out at this country station. With each one of them in turn nodding to the ticket collector, they made their way off the platform, out of the station and in crocodile fashion up and out of sight. As suddenly as the platform had filled, it emptied and with a wave of the green flag and the sound of the Guard's whistle, the train pulled out of the station and continued its journey northwards to Manchester.

Two fresh faced rookie Wrens stood on an empty platform and looked at each other.

"Hello. My name is Charlotte. Most people call me Charlie."

"Hello, I'm Bobbie, only me Mam calls us Roberta."

The girls laughed. This was the beginning of a very special friendship.

HMS Pembroke V

September 1942

CHARLIE AND BOBBIE SAT AT MRS JONES' KITCHEN TABLE eating home-made scones and strawberry jam. They had been at Bletchley Park for six weeks and had quite literally been thrown in at the deep end. After arriving on that August afternoon the two girls had both been allocated their temporary billet with Mr and Mrs Jones in nearby Simpson village and been told to report for duty at 0800 hours the following morning to start their training.

On their first day on board HMS Pembroke V, as Bletchley Park was known in naval terms, Charlie had been taken into a room in Hut 8, introduced to her watch and placed in front of what looked like an over sized typewriting machine set on its own table. Girls were sitting quietly setting their machines, reading from a sheet of paper and typing onto long thin strips of paper. Charlie had looked in horror at the contraption in front of her in the realisation that she was going to be a typist sitting in an office all day.

"Don't worry, you'll soon get used to it," said the girl sitting at the machine next to hers, "My name's Joan, I'll show you what to do."

Joan started to explain how the machine worked. Taking one of the messages from the tray she selected the drums, plugged up the board as indicated then placed the sheet of paper on the stand above the keyboard.

"Here you are, you can start typing now," she said.

Charlie looked in dismay. The sheet of paper was full of lines with jumbled letters split into groups of five. She turned to Joan and said, "So I just type these letters?"

"Yes, then once you recognise a German word appearing on the paper strip you stop, raise your hand and have it checked. If it's OK you carry on."

Charlie's heart sank. Not only was she going to be a typist sitting in an office all day; she was going to be reading German!

Meanwhile in Hut 11 Bobbie had been greeted by the heat, noise and the smell of machinery and was introduced to Doreen and the machine called Agnus. Bobbie had been put under Doreen's wing to be trained on site. Though this was slightly unusual both Wrens knew to take orders and most certainly did not ask questions.

Hut 11 was home to six Bombe machines each standing six feet six inches high, seven feet four inches long and two feet five inches wide. Bobbie looked in dismay at the two rows of machines each with their moving drums clicking round, the oil trays beneath them and the mass of wires and plugs behind.

"Don't worry," Doreen shouted above the noise, "you'll soon get used to it."

Bobbie thought, "If only you knew pet, I didn't want to work wi' machines!"

Doreen set up the Bombe machine, and Bobbie began to learn from an excellent teacher. That was just six weeks ago and both Charlie and Bobbie had learned quickly, though neither told the other what they did. They went to work together and they came back to their billet together to be greeted by Mrs Jones, her home cooking, fresh clean bedding and a hot bath every Friday. They shared a bedroom and slept in the luxury of soft beds, not bunks.

HMS Pembroke V

Mr Jones had kindly fixed up two old bicycles which, on their days and evenings off, gave the girls the independence of their own personal transport. They cycled along to the County Cinema in Fenny Stratford, or back to the railway station at Bletchley where they piled their bikes into the Guard's van and made their way to Bedford, Oxford or Cambridge for the day. Other times they simply enjoyed the freedom of cycling along the canal tow path, taking in the fresh air and making the most of those last days of summer. Under the strict instructions from Mr Jones the girls were told never to use the tow path at night, and could be heard singing and laughing as they peddled along the dark country lanes.

This was in sharp contrast to the underlying tensions they felt on board HMS Pembroke V, particularly in Hut 8. When Charlie had signed the Official Secrets Act she was told she would be working on enemy codes and had soon begun to understand the importance of the task she was given, which at first had seemed so mundane and repetitive. She was a proficient typist and had quickly mastered the typing machine contraption she now knew to be a Type-X machine, one of the machines modified to imitate an Enigma machine. She had proven her abilities to identify the formation of German words in the continuous string of letters that she typed out on the thin strip of paper. She didn't bat an eye at the use of German slang, and had long since ceased to blush at their use of rude language. She had even begun to develop a knack of recognising the writing styles and limited vocabulary of the senders.

Yet, whilst she knew they were reading some messages she sensed the pressure and frustration which began to affect everyone as they fought to break back into German Naval Enigma. She had caught a glimpse of the two young men who had shared her train compartment, huddled over sheets of paper in deep discussion. She had heard raised voices coming from behind closed doors. She had registered the silent despair at each report of the German U-boats hunting alone, or in wolf-packs; picking off merchant, commercial and naval ships at will; sending them and their cargos to the bottom of the Atlantic Ocean, indiscriminately killing men, women and children.

Over in Hut 11 Bobbie had proven her abilities working on the Bombe machines. She had soon got used to the incessant noise and the smell of oil, which she likened to a busy day in Mr Heppell's garage, and Doreen had said she was a natural, whatever that had meant. Bobbie had soon discovered that the original Bombe operators were RAF mechanics as it had not been considered a job for women, but with those men needed elsewhere Wrens were brought in. Doreen was one of the first of the group of Wrens drafted into Bletchley Park to operate the machines and apart from a short training session from someone who came over from Letchworth, she had learned on the job and quickly risen through the ranks to Petty Officer. Each machine had a name and Agnus was Doreen's favourite because, as she said, it was the first machine she had ever worked on. The boffins had given it some Latin name, Agnus Dei, but Doreen much preferred Agnus and chastised anyone, regardless of rank, who further shortened it to Aggie.

Initially Bobbie was unaware of the importance of her job which was helping those in Hut 6 to break into German Army and Air Force Enigma messages but it was the messages they could not break from the German Navy through Hut 8 which caused frustration all round; even in Hut 11.

Though Charlie and Bobbie had made friends on their watch it was no surprise that in those early days of settling in they both appreciated the comfort of the Jones' cottage and the couple's kindness. There was nothing quite like sitting in Mrs Jones' kitchen eating her home made scones and strawberry jam, knowing that they had the whole of the following day to do as they wished.

Daintily licking the jam from her fingers and looking up at the ceiling, Charlie posed the question, "What shall we do tomorrow Bobbie?"

"Sleep?" replied Bobbie slipping her shoes off and putting her feet up on the chair opposite.

"No, we cannot do that. We should go somewhere. Go for a walk," replied Charlie.

"Oh no pet, I've been on us feet all week," winced Bobbie as she rubbed her ankles.

"We could go on a cycle ride then," suggested Charlie, "even though I have been sat on my backside all week!"

"OK, but not too far pet, we don't want you to get a sore bum now do we?" teased Bobbie.

The two girls laughed, cleared the table, washed their dishes and went upstairs to get out of their uniforms and settle down for a lazy evening and an early night.

The following morning they woke to the smell of freshly baked bread. Even in this time of rationing there was always plenty of good plain food to eat at the Jones' and the girls knew how lucky they were. Mrs Jones was an excellent cook and seemed to make a feast out of next to nothing. Mr Jones tended to his chickens, fruit trees and well stocked vegetable garden, and when Charlie's mother sent her weekly food parcels they all shared the bounty of tins of biscuits, spam and salmon, though Mrs Jones was at a loss as to what she should do with the caviar. Charlie always phoned her mother from the local telephone box to thank her for the parcels but never dared ask where she got the food from.

So, on that September morning, secure in the comfort of their beds the two girls lay chatting for a while and planning their day. They would ask Mrs Jones if they could take a picnic and make the short cycle ride along the canal tow path up to the Red Lion at Fenny Lock and watch the highly decorated canal barges wind their way up and down the Grand Junction Canal. There was also a good chance of meeting some of the other 'Simpsons' at the canal side pub enjoying their day off. Like most of the villages around Bletchley, Simpson was a war-time home to a number of Bletchley Park people. With those billeted in the village known as 'the Simpsons', it had not taken long for both Charlie and Bobbie to become known as the 'Simpson girls'.

With their day planned they went downstairs for breakfast. Mrs Jones had set the table for two and tucked the letter under Bobbie's plate before going out into the garden to help her husband with their autumn harvest. Seeing her Mam's neat handwriting peeping out from under the clean white crockery, Bobbie rushed over to the table, eagerly ripped open the envelope and began to read the letter out loud.

My dear Roberta,

I am sorry to say pet that we have some very sad news and I think you should sit down before you read this letter. I am hoping that you get this before you find out from anywhere else. Your Cousin Peter has been reported missing presumed killed. He was in a convoy sailing back from America to Liverpool when the u-boat hit. Your Da says Peter would have stayed by his radio even as his ship went down. What a brave lad.

Since your Aunt Jayne got the telegram she has been beside herself with grief, losing your Uncle Jack and now Peter. The whole village has been worried about her so Mr Heppell drove your Dad over to Whitley Bay to collect her and bring her back here to stay up at Prospect House with your Ma and Da.

Mr Heppell has been very kind and would not take a penny for the journey so your Dad is making him a radio set in one of his nice cabinets.

Take care pet and always remember what your Ma says. Some people come into our lives and quickly go, others stay a while and leave footprints on our hearts and we are never, ever the same.

I will close now as your Dad is going to take this letter to the post for me.

Your ever loving
Mam and Dad xx

{ 7 }

The Letter

BOBBIE SANK INTO HER CHAIR. Tears filled her eyes, and the letter drifted to the floor. Through blurred vision she stared into the distant past which was once her youth, and felt Peter's footprint on her heart.

Charlie stood motionless by the kitchen door and was suddenly reminded of the stark reality of war that she had blocked from her mind. Then, moving over to the table she picked up the letter from the floor, took her friend in her arms and shared her pain. Locked in that time warp known only by those who have been touched by grief; the two girls wept.

As if from out of no-where Mrs Jones had made a pot of tea, set it on the kitchen table, dusted down the half bottle of brandy from the dresser and placed it next to two of her best glasses. Glancing up at the photograph of the young man in uniform, and with the unspoken respect of one who knew only too well that time-warp of grief, she wiped a tear from her eye and retreated to the garden to join her husband.

Charlie's Story

Charlie was all too aware of the dangers of crossing the Atlantic Ocean. April 1940 had marked the end of the Phoney War and with the German invasion of Denmark and Norway, Charlie's father had decided that she and her mother should go to Canada to join her aunt in Montreal. Her mother's protests had fallen on deaf ears and on 26th June 1940, both mother and daughter boarded the *S.S. Duchess of Athol* in Liverpool bound for Quebec and Montreal. Charlie was excited, she had only made the short trips on a steamer across the English Channel to spent her school holidays with her parents in France when her father had been working in the British Embassy in Paris; and the thought of nearly two weeks on board a luxury liner, crossing the Atlantic Ocean, was certainly going to be quite an adventure.

Arriving in Liverpool, Charlie and her mother had spent the night in the splendour of the *Midland*

Adelphi Hotel, which at the time was considered the most fashionable of Atlantic stop-over's, frequented by royalty, film stars and prime ministers. The following day they had boarded their Ocean liner and Charlie was pleasantly surprised to see so many children and young people. Making friends with a group of girls from Sherborne Girls' School, she suddenly realised that just like her, they were all being evacuated. Though the Sherborne girls were travelling with their teachers, many like her were travelling with their mothers; some children were accompanied by their nannies or older siblings whilst others, including toddlers and babies, were travelling alone in the care of the ship's stewards.

Naturally, there was much emotion as the Canadian Pacific liner left Liverpool docks to join the rest of its convoy under the protection of the Royal Navy battleship and make its way into open sea. Though Charlie shared a cabin with her mother she spent most of her time with the girls from Sherborne playing deck games, mustering for life-boat drill and taking instructions as what to do in the event of a torpedo attack. Yet all too soon, their fantasy of youthful adventure turned into the reality of war.

Whilst still in the perceived safety of home waters and within sight of land, they had watched as two RAF aircraft circled over the convoy before dropping bombs into the sea. Little did they know the bombs had hit their target, a German submarine skulking in the icy waters intent on sending the *S.S. Duchess of Athol* and its passengers to the bottom of the sea. They had heard the eerie sounds of the ships' horns as the convoy cut its way through the Atlantic fog. They had woken one morning to find the convoy in tight formation with the battleship tucked in alongside them, close enough for them to hear the orders issued to those on deck, and to see the sailors manning the guns. They had heard the sound of depth charges and felt the terror grip those passengers on board as the ship pitched and reeled. They saw mothers, concealing their own fears, cradling their children against the unknown. In turn Charlie and her mother had tried desperately to comfort those children travelling alone, and had listened to the reassuring message from the ship's Captain confirming that they had successfully frightened off a 'porpoise' which had found its way between the ships' convoy.

Nearly two long weeks after leaving Liverpool and zigzagging across that vast expanse of the Atlantic Ocean the mood on board the *S.S. Duchess of Athol* became more relaxed as their vessel reached the safety of the St Lawrence River and made its way inland to Quebec and then on to Montreal. Even as the tension eased, neither Charlie, her mother, or the rest of the passengers were aware of the danger they had been in, and how the Captain and his crew, the Royal Air Force bombers and the Royal Navy battleship had shielded them from the German U-boats which had been stalking them, intent on sending them to the bottom of the Ocean.

Reaching Montreal, Charlie's mother cabled her husband to say that they had arrived safely; they were settling into the comfortable rented house and had found a suitable school for Charlotte to complete her final year of education when, as she most definitely stated, they would both be returning to England. Charlie's mother had not taken kindly to being packed off to Canada and had decided to treat it as a vacation, and where Charlie could improve her French. With the start of the new term Charlie soon settled into day school, and both mother and daughter were enjoying each other's company when news of the sinking of the *S.S, City of Benares* hit.

In September 1940, just like the *S.S. Duchess of Athol* and the *S.S. Duchess of Bedford* had done so many months before, the *S.S. City of Benares* had joined its convoy and left Liverpool bound for Quebec and Montreal carrying 407 passengers and crew, including its precious load of 90 children being evacuated to the safety of Canada. Just before midnight on the 17th September 1940, and four days into sailing the convoy was spotted by the German U-boat, *U-48*. The Captain gave the order to fire two torpedoes. They missed their target. Sixteen minutes later at one minute past midnight on the 18th September the *U-48* fired a third torpedo which hit its target and within thirty minutes the *S.S. City of Benares* sank 253 miles west south-west of Rockall, taking with it 260 lives including 77 of the 90 evacuee children.

Back in London, as a direct result of the media outcry the Children's Overseas Reception Board ceased sending children across the Atlantic. Whilst in Montreal, Charlie and her mother felt the fear and the pain, and in their minds heard the cries of the children and grieved for those they had never met. With the mixed emotions of anger, outrage and the guilt of their own safe crossing, both mother and daughter were even more determined that once Charlie had finished her education they would both return to England.

So as agreed, in the autumn of 1941 and in somewhat safer waters, Charlie and her mother crossed the Atlantic Ocean once again and returned home to war torn England. At the time, little did Charlie know that within months she would be working in the very place, and with the very group of people who, in 1941 had managed to break into German Naval Enigma messages and for a short period of time had made the Atlantic crossings safer. Nor did she realise that within a year, she too would be part of that same team battling to break into the German U-boat Enigma messages.

Bobbie's Story

Unlike Charlie, Bobbie had never even crossed the English Channel, let alone an Ocean. The closest that she had got to the sea was when she visited her Cousin Peter and Aunt Jayne in Whitley Bay and had paddled in the waters of the North Sea as it lapped against the sandy shores of the Northumbrian coast.

After Peter's Dad had died her Aunt Jayne had kept house for West Cornforth's widowed doctor, and on his retirement from the village practice he had decided to move to the coast. He had bought a large town house in Whitley Bay overlooking the sea and had asked Aunt Jayne if she would continue to be his housekeeper and join him. Though her Aunt had been reluctant to leave the village she finally agreed and together with Peter she moved into a self contained flat in the doctor's town house. Dr Foster had no children of his own but he welcomed the sound of children playing and enjoyed their company, and Bobbie spent her school holidays by the seaside staying with her Aunt and her Cousin

The Letter

Peter. During those summers of the 1930s the two young cousins enjoyed many adventures together, spending their days on the North Sea coast between Seaton Sluice and Cullercoats Bay where, in the innocence of youth, they were totally oblivious of what lurked over the dark horizon.

Peter was older than Bobbie and all too soon their long summer holidays came to an end when he left school and joined the General Post Office, as an apprentice working in the Coastal Radio Station at Cullercoats. So with his new found love of the sea and knowledge of radio, it was no surprise to Bobbie that on the outbreak of war Peter volunteered to join the Royal Navy and become a telegraphist.

The last time the two cousins had met on that winter's evening, Peter had confided in Bobbie that he was scared his luck would run out. He had crossed the Atlantic before, always in convoy and had seen ships picked off like sitting ducks by the invisible menace of the German U-boats as if, in that vast stretch of Ocean, they knew exactly where to find them. As a radio operator he had picked up the distress signals of other vessels and kept contact with them as ships went to their rescue, scooping survivors from the icy waters of the Atlantic. He was haunted by those final messages and the deadly silence as both ship and men went down and, as if he already knew his fate, he had hugged his little cousin tight as they had said their goodbyes

With five other members of the Royal Navy and eight gunners of the Royal Artillery, Peter joined the ship's commodore and his crew of merchant seamen aboard the *M.V. Athelsultan*, and set sail from Liverpool across the Atlantic Ocean. On its return journey from Port Everglades, Florida it joined Convoy *SC-100* when at 0019 hours central European time on the 23rd September 1942 it was targeted by the German *U 617*. The torpedo hit its mark and within minutes the tanker, with its cargo of molasses and alcohol sank, taking fifty-one of the sixty-one ships complement with it.

Bobbie would never know what really happened to Peter. Nor would she realise the part she would play in the eventual capture of the *U-617* the following September.

Locked in thought the two friends sat, drank tea and sipped Mrs Jones' brandy, and like many other women working at Bletchley Park they quickly learned to conceal their grief. Shielded beneath their own veil of secrecy of untold knowledge they both returned to HMS Pembroke V the following morning, even more determined to play their part in the secret battle of the dark, deep cold waters of the North Atlantic.

{ 8 }

Battle against Time

Breaking the Cipher

BLETCHLEY PARK NEVER SLEPT and in those dark days of 1942 the pressure on Hut 8 to break back into the German Naval Enigma continued. Without that vital intelligence gleaned from those messages, the German Navy and in particular their U-boats were once again in command of the seas. The Wrens worked three eight hour watches, six days on and one day off. Each week the watches shifted around the twenty-four hour clock and those on afternoon and night watches went back to their billets to sleep through the day and work through the long dark evenings and night. Civilians too worked shifts around the clock, though with the comparative freedom of civilian life, many often chose to sleep on make shift camp beds, cat-napping before resuming their battle against time. During those short daylight hours of autumn the brick bomb blast-walls, built around the wooden huts for protection, also blocked out the daylight. Yet out of the diverse shadows of despair came a shaft of light.

On 30th October 1942, as the Simpson girls were getting ready to start their watch aboard HMS Pembroke V, over in the Mediterranean Sea three British seamen left the comparative safety of the British destroyer *HMS Petard* to board the captured stricken German U-boat *U-559*. Entering the abandoned and sinking vessel Lieutenant Tony Fasson RN and Able Seaman Colin Grazier seized German documents and charts which they handed to Petard's young NAAFI canteen assistant Tommy Brown. As Brown returned to *HMS Petard* with their prized pinch, the *U-559* sank and the two British sailors still on board paid the ultimate price. Their selfless actions marked a turning point, giving the code-breakers of Bletchley Park the intelligence they needed to help them break back into German U-boat Enigma and scuttle the wolf-packs.

The news of the pinch echoed across the airwaves and was met in Hut 8 with a mix of silence, disbelief, euphoria then the rush of all hands on deck, and as autumn slipped into winter the mood in Huts 4, 8 and 11 lightened, though their work load increased. Somehow it didn't matter that the girls did not see the light of day for what seemed like weeks on end, or that they shivered from cold as the icicles formed on huts and buildings across the Park. Even if they did not know exactly what they were doing, there was now an unspoken sense of achievement and a boost in morale. At the end of their watch on those dark nights and cold mornings they met up outside Hut 11 and walked past the tennis courts to catch their transport parked by the lake. Cold, tired and hungry they sat on the hard wooden seats of the charabanc as their driver followed route number 3 to take them on their short journey to the comfort, warmth and hospitality of the Jones' cottage and a sleep of contentment after a job well done.

Both girls knew they were very lucky and that not all billets were as comfortable as theirs and as Christmas approached Charlie became more and more concerned about the health of the scruffy young man she had met on the train that bright August afternoon. No matter what time of day or night she was on duty, he always seemed to be there. He looked tired and drawn and Charlie had soon realised why he was so unkempt. He was one of those university types who rarely went back to their billet and often worked night and day, in what appeared to be his own personal battle against time. He had developed an awful cough, his jacket hung around his shoulders and Charlie was sure he was losing weight.

In the only way possible, in that secret place, Charlie had confided her concerns to Bobbie about a tired young man who just might benefit from some decent food. With their fingers crossed behind their backs they asked Mrs Jones if she could perhaps put something together from Charlie's mother's food parcel for a particularly sickly looking Wren who was in a bad billet. With somewhat of a knowing smile Mrs Jones immediately raided her pantry, ignoring the ever increasing stock of caviar, and took out a tin of spam, a loaf of bread and promptly made a stack of man sized sandwiches. Together with a large piece of her fruit cake and an apple from one of the trees in the garden, she popped them into a brown paper bag for Charlie to give to their 'friend'.

The following morning, it was no surprise to Charlie that as soon as she walked into Hut 8 she met the young man in the corridor. Making a feeble excuse about her landlady overfeeding her, she clumsily thrust the paper bag into his hand. The young man smiled and gratefully accepted the gift before disappearing into his office and gently closing the door behind him. Charlie would never see the young man again.

{ 9 }

Home on Leave

Christmas 1942

JUST FOUR MONTHS AFTER MEETING ON BLETCHLEY RAILWAY STATION the two girls stood on opposite platforms waiting for their trains. It was Christmas Eve and both girls were on leave making their way to spend the festive season with their families, and as the northbound train approached, Bobbie waved goodbye to her friend. Having discharged its usual load of passengers onto the station's platform, Bobbie boarded the train, found herself a seat by the window and settled down for the long journey home.

Home on Leave

Somewhere near Durham

It had taken a whole day for Bobbie to make the journey from Bletchley via Crewe up to Manchester where she changed trains to Darlington scheduled to stop at Ferry Hill Junction. She had waited until she crossed over to Manchester Victoria Station and was well settled on the Darlington train before she tucked into the spam sandwiches and fruit cake Mrs Jones had packed for her. It was then she found the tins of caviar with the note from Mrs Jones saying, "Bobbie, will your Mam know what to do with these?"

On arriving at Ferry Hill Station Bobbie had been relieved that she needn't telephone 52 West Cornforth, Mr Heppell's garage, as both her Dad and Mr Heppell were sitting on the platform waiting for her. Tired and cold she snuggled next to her Dad in the back of Mr Heppell's car and on their short journey over to West Cornforth, slept the sleep of a child, safe and content in the sanctuary of family and friends.

Christmas Day was nice and quiet, just her and her Mam and Dad. They had enjoyed her Mam's good cooking, listened to the King's speech on her Dad's radio set and sat up late into the night chatting by the roaring coal fire. No-one mentioned the war.

On Boxing Day her Mam had organised a family get together and put on a lovely spread. It would seem everyone had pooled their rations and Great Aunt Edith had brought one of her specialities from the big house; game pie. Da provided the ham and peas-pudding and Aunt Jayne and Ma had been busy for weeks making cakes and preserves. Mam had asked Bobbie if she could give the tins of caviar to Great Aunt Edith to take back up to the big house, as only she would know what to do with them. Bobbie readily agreed and everyone was satisfied the well travelled tins would at last go to a good home. Throughout the day friends and neighbours popped in to say hello and they all said how well Bobbie looked. They even commented on how the sea air must be doing her good. Thinking of the confines and noise of Hut 11, Bobbie smiled and agreed secretly thinking, "If only you knew".

Somewhere in London

Meanwhile down in London Charlie had arrived at Euston Station where her father had sent a car and driver to collect her. Her parents were renting a flat in Queen Anne's Gate very close to her father's office and, as he was on call most of the time, it was easier for her mother to stay in London with him. It also meant that she could maintain her social calendar and keep abreast of things. Her mother had enjoyed a good life and travelled the world with her husband. She found the war tiresome and since her visit to Canada, she was even more determined not to give in to what she called, "that Austrian upstart who thought himself a German".

On Christmas Day Charlie and her parents dined at the *Dorchester* which her mother believed to be one of the safest buildings in London. The fact that Mr Churchill stayed there and earlier that year the American General Eisenhower had swapped his allegiance from *Claridge's* to take a suite at the *Dorchester Hotel*, endorsed that belief. There was also that added attraction of bumping into fellow diners like T.S. Eliot, Harold Nicolson and Edith Sitwell, whose literary work Charlie's mother so admired.

Later that afternoon the family returned to their flat and spent the evening sipping brandy and chatting when Charlie's father asked, "Well my dear Charlotte, tell me. What are things really like in the country?"

Both father and daughter exchanged discerning glances. Nothing more was said, nor indeed needed to be said.

On Boxing Day Charlie's mother had organised a cocktail party in Charlie's honour. Charlie was approaching marriageable age and her mother was determined to find her daughter a suitable husband.

There was a rather nice young man from an excellent background working in her husband's office who she thought would fit the bill. As the cocktail hour rapidly approached people, whom Charlie had never met before, began arriving at the flat. Her mother, as always, was the perfect hostess and likewise Charlie circulated the room making sure she spent time with each of the guests, all of whom seemed to be her parent's age or much older. Charlie had just excused herself from the company of one elderly Major when her mother came up behind her and whispered, "Charlotte dear, I would like to introduce you to William. I understand he works with your father in the Foreign Office."

With her back to their guest Charlie flexed her muscles in an attempt to loosen the stiff smile which had become engraved on her face. Then taking a deep breath she turned and locked eyes with the most handsome man she had seen in yonks.

"Oh. Good Lord!" she exclaimed.

The young man looked taken aback, "No sorry. Not yet, may be one day!"

"Pardon?" questioned Charlie.

"I am not a Lord yet. Does that matter?" said the young man.

"Most definitely not," replied Charlie and digging her size five feet even further into the quagmire continued, "I just expected you to be older."

"I'm not making much of an impression here then am I?" teased the young man.

"No, no. No of course not!" protested Charlie, then lowering her voice and glancing furtively around the room she whispered, "I am trying to get away from them!"

The two young people laughed and to her mother's delight Charlie remained engaged in conversation with William for the rest of the evening.

New Year's Eve 1942

All too soon the girls' leave was over and on New Year's Eve they each made their separate ways back to Simpson, and their second home. Charlie had returned from London with her kit bag and her old school trunk which her mother had packed full of the necessities of life. As the trunk was 'far too heavy' for Charlotte to lift, her mother had deemed it fit to arrange that both Charlotte and her belongings be returned to her country billet by motor car. Luckily, one of Charlotte's father's colleagues, just happened to be visiting the area, and her transport was organised. William collected Charlie from Queen Anne's Gate.

Later that day, when the motor car pulled up outside Rose Cottage, the inhabitants of Simpson village twitched their lace curtains as the handsome young city couple got out of the car and off loaded a large trunk and a kit bag into Mrs Jones' front parlour. William stayed for a cup of tea and piece of Mrs Jones' fruit cake before leaving to make his way on to his next port of call.

Meanwhile, Bobbie had spent her day squeezed in smoky overcrowded trains and when she finally arrived at Bletchley Station too late to catch the evening transport to Simpson, she decided to cross over the platform and see if she could hitch a lift in the Guard's van of the Whitehall, the special war train which ferried the code-breakers between Bletchley and Bedford. Relieved to see that Ted was on duty she smiled sweetly and asked if he could take her in his Guard's van that one stop along the line to Fenny Stratford, from where she could walk the extra mile down the lane to Simpson.

He had agreed and as the train pulled into Fenny Station, Ted lifted Bobbie's bags down onto the platform and wished his travelling companion a Happy New Year, before blowing hard on his whistle and waving his train onwards. As the locomotive chugged off into the darkness, leaving Bobbie surrounded by the cold stillness of a winter's night, she wondered if she had really made the right decision to walk down the spooky lane to Simpson alone.

Taking a deep breath, she picked up her bags and her courage and making her way off the station platform heard a familiar strain of a motor car engine refusing to start. Focusing her eyes in the darkness she saw the vehicle with its bonnet open and a figure of a man bending over the engine.

"Hello," she shouted, "are you alright. Do you need a hand?"

"Oh, gosh!" the man said with a start, bashing his head on the car's bonnet as he got up. "Didn't see you there. Not sure you can really. The damn thing's just spluttered to a halt. Won't start. Good job it stopped here and not up there," nodding towards the level crossing, "It could have been a bit nasty in the blackout."

Bobbie agreed and walking over to the car put her bags down and asked, "Have you got a torch in your glove box?"

"Oh. Not sure. It's not my car."

Bobbie gave the man a sideways glance and frowned.

"Oh. Sorry. Not my car. Borrowed you see. Never driven the damn thing before." explained the man.

Bobbie reached into the glove box, found the torch and went to look under the bonnet. She then moved back into the car and sat in the driver's seat and pushing the over-extended choke back in, put her foot firmly down on the accelerator pedal and turned the key. With a spurt the engine burst back to life. In the dim torch light she saw a look of amazement on the man's face as he muttered, "How the hell did you do that?"

Then, immediately apologising for his language he said, "You are an Angel."

Bobbie smiled and replied, "No, not yet I hope; may be one day."

They both laughed.

"You'd flooded the engine. It's easily done if you don't know the car," said Bobbie not wishing to embarrass the man further.

Then, making sure the engine was ticking over nicely she pulled down the bonnet, returned the torch to the glove box, picked up her bags, wished the man a Happy New Year and turned to make her way down the lane.

"Wait a minute," the man called out, "Where are you going? Can I give you a lift? It is the least I can do."

"That's alright. I'm going the other way."

"I can turn the car around you know. I'm not that stupid," he teased.

They laughed again.

"Yes, thank you. That'd be nice. It's not far but it's a bit scary at night on us own."

"Come on then, hop in," he said as he took Bobbie's bags and put them in the car's trunk. Revving the engine ever so slightly, he turned the car around and they drove down the dark lane towards Simpson. As they reached the Plough public house Bobbie said she could get out and walk from there. They thanked each other for the help and went their separate ways. As the man pulled away Bobbie walked the short distance towards St. Thomas' church and the Jones' cottage and she did not hear him say, "Good-night my Angel."

The Jones' had spent a quiet Christmas without the two girls and when both returned bearing gifts and news, the Jones' cottage once again vibrated with the sound of youthful laughter. Charlie had waited until Bobbie arrived before opening her trunk to see what her mother had packed, and with Charlie's trunk and Bobbie's suitcase in the Jones' front parlour, both girls eagerly investigated the contents.

Charlie's mother had thought that her daughter had looked 'a bit peaky' and there was a substantial amount of rouge, lipstick, face powder and night cream. Horrified at the sight of Charlotte's shapely legs hidden under rough navy issue lisle stockings, her mother had purchased half a dozen boxes of the latest American style fully fashioned nylon stockings which had been delivered, at a price, to the London flat by a very shifty looking fellow wearing an over sized raincoat. Navy issue knickers were another matter which Charlie's mother felt the need to address. She had packed a number of silk chemise, slips and knickers she deemed much more suitable to be worn under the afternoon dresses she had carefully folded in tissue paper and placed in individual boxes. As a seasoned traveler, Charlie's mother had always found silk to be most accommodating. There was also a food hamper containing the usual tins together with a selection of cheeses and a picnic basket with four settings of crockery, cutlery, champagne flutes, a tablecloth and napkins.

Bobbie's gifts were equally useful. Her Mam had knitted a range of woolly hats, socks and mittens. Bobbie's Mam could manage to knit thumbs but adding four fingers of varying lengths proved far too fiddly and she maintained that hands kept much warmer in mittens anyway. Bobbie agreed. Even as a child she had failed to fit her tiny fingers into the twisted appendages of her Mam's knitted gloves and had formed a fist in the palms, letting the fingers stand up like the plume of her Dad's cockerel. Aunt Jayne had crocheted a pair of multi coloured blankets, unable to break a habit of a lifetime making two of everything. Her Da had neatly folded a crisp white £5 note and pressed it into Bobbie's hand as they said goodbye. He had always been astute and the rent that he received for the telegraph poles sited on his land was put aside for his only grand-daughter on such occasions. Bobbie's Dad had apologised that he could not finish her present in time, 'as he had run out of parts' and would send it on later. In the meantime he had given her his big Bakelite torch which he thought would come in handy. Great Aunt Edith had packed a game pie and her Mam had sent some ham and peas-pudding back for supper.

So it was on 31st December, as 1942 drew to a close, Mrs Jones took down the remaining brandy from the dresser, polished four of her best glasses and laid them on the table next to the game pie, ham, cheese peas-pudding and freshly made bread. On the stroke of midnight, each with their own thoughts, they raised their glasses to absent friends, loved ones and to their hopes for 1943.

{ 10 }

Sea of Change

Moving On

BACK ON BOARD HMS PEMBROKE V CHANGES WERE AFOOT. The October pinch which had enabled Hut 8 to break back into the German U-boat Enigma also brought other challenges with increased demands on the Bombe machines and personnel. Four additional properties were requisitioned at Adstock, Gayhurst, Stanmore and Wavendon, with buildings to house the extra Bombe machines and to provide the on-site living quarters for the increased numbers of Wrens being drafted in to run them. Doreen, now a Chief Wren and one of the more experienced Bombe operators, left Hut 11 to take up her new moorings at Stanmore where provision was being made for 750 Wrens to serve.

Bobbie too had been given her orders to move and was relieved to find that she only need make the much shorter journey from Hut 11 to its extension, Hut 11a tucked behind the back gardens of the Stable Yard cottages. Her skills as a Bombe operator and mechanic had quickly been identified so when the Hut 11a machines were designated to include training and experimental work as well as ordinary operations, Bobbie was the obvious choice.

With winter drawing to a close those working in Huts 4 and 8 completed their move from the stuffy wooden huts to purpose built brick buildings, taking with them their hut identification numbers. There was a little more comfort in their new abode and though the girls sat on hard wooden chairs and worked on sturdy trestle tables there was still the need for black out curtains at night. However, in the daytime the large windows let in light, fresh air and for some, a view over the lake or what remained of the Leon's gardens. Most of Charlie's watch had moved over to the new buildings but she had not seen the scruffy young man since before Christmas and she was not surprised to hear that he had reported sick.

The Navy, as always, was concerned about health, and it had been clear for some time that not all working and living conditions on board HMS Pembroke V were conducive to good health. Large groups of people working in close confinement in dingy, airless, stuffy or smoke filled rooms was giving rise to an increase in highly infectious diseases including influenza, pneumonia and tuberculosis. Not all billets were satisfactory and the Navy decided for reasons of health and cost that Wrens stationed at Bletchley Park would be allocated living quarters and the Admiralty requisitioned a number of country houses in the area for that purpose.

So, when Bobbie and Charlie finally received their orders to move out of their temporary billet in Simpson and into quarters at Crawley Grange they were pleased to be going to the same place but sad to leave the Jones'. Mr and Mrs Jones were both equally upset to lose their girls and Mr Jones said they could keep the bicycles and Mrs Jones said they could visit anytime. Charlie left the contents of her mother's latest food parcel in the safe keeping of Mrs Jones to do with as she wished, though the ever increasing stock of caviar was proving a challenge.

The Simpson girls had managed to organise their move to Crawley Grange on their four days off work, and with the Bletchley Park transport route to North

Crawley going through Simpson village they had arranged to pick up the early morning charabanc taking the night-watch back to their quarters in the Grange. Mrs Jones had made her usual tuck bags of food to take with them and Mr Jones had promised to deliver their bicycles, Bobbie's suitcase and Charlie's trunk over to Crawley Grange the following day. With the promise to be back soon, and with kit bags and Aunt Jayne's crochet blankets over their arms, Bobbie and Charlie boarded their transport and waved farewell to the Jones'.

The mood on the charabanc was unusually quiet and Charlie and Bobbie thought the other Wrens looked somewhat pale huddled beneath their own personal blankets. Grateful for the lift and with an understanding nod they made their way to take up their seats at the rear of the bus. However, it soon became clear that all on board were sitting, not in the silence of the exhaustion of five nights on watch, but trepidation as the charabanc bounced its way over the hump back canal bridge and lurched along the Newport Road, frightening a group of young children congregated outside the Simpson School.

Leaving the comparative comfort of the villages behind them, the driver headed out into the countryside towards Newport Pagnell where she stopped and made frequent references to the dog eared road map that Mr Budd, Bletchley Park's transport manager had given her just two hours earlier. After passing the same farm house for the third time, one of the Wrens staggered to the front of the bus and issued directions, suggesting that on their arrival in North Crawley they disembark on the High Street and that they walk from there. This suggestion was gratefully received by one and all, including the driver, as the Wrens reached their destination and tumbled off the charabanc. Collecting their belongings Charlie and Bobbie followed and in her usual manner, trying to avoid embarrassment at all times, Bobbie smiled and touching their driver's arm said, "Thanks pet, it's been an interestin' trip."

To which the ashen faced driver simply replied, "I'm glad."

From that moment on the ATS driver became affectionately known as 'Gladys' and her charabanc was called 'HMS Trepidation'.

Once Gladys had been given reverse instructions to navigate 'HMS Trepidation' back to its moorings at Bletchley Park her passengers all wished her well, waved her goodbye and wondered if she would ever be seen again.

Sea of Change

Charlie and Bobbie joined the weary night-watch as they walked along the High Street, into Pond Lane and turned down the tree lined drive which led to Crawley Grange. On emerging from the cover of the trees the two girls were met by a sight which quite literally took their breath away. The magnificent country house, with its mullioned windows, gable ends and individual decorative tall brick chimneys was the essence of original Tudor design, and believed to have been one of the homes of Cardinal Wolsey.

As would have been expected of any Cardinal, Lord Chancellor or dignitary of the time, the house came with an estate befitting a man akin to Wolsey's power and position. Regardless of the politics of sixteenth century England under the Tudor King, Henry VIII and the downfall of Wolsey, Crawley Grange had most certainly stood the test of time

Entering the house the girls adjusted their eyes from the sharp daylight of early spring, to the dark interior of the main hall lit by the warmth of the orange and red flames of the log fire crackling in the large grate. The house had been requisitioned from the Boswell family, who had subsequently taken up residence on North Crawley's High Street, and any secret fears the Simpson girls may have had about their move from the Jones' had disappeared. They both knew that, in a different sort of way, they would be equally happy at Crawley Grange. As the night-watch made its way to the kitchen for breakfast Chief Petty Officer Lillian Ashley escorted Charlie and Bobbie up the grand Elizabethan staircase to their cabin at the front of the house.

Charlie had been used to large dormitories and the community life at boarding school whereas Bobbie had not, and had welcomed the familiarity of their Simpson billet. However, their new quarters provided them with the best of both worlds, a small cabin with two bunk beds, plenty of space to socialise in the Mess and access to beautiful countryside.

After stowing their kit the two Wrens went to explore the house. As some of the rooms were locked and staircases were roped off the girls were careful not to disturb the night-watch as they settled down in their cabins and soon realised that they had the smallest cabin,

There was definitely no shortage of toilets or bathrooms however, there were rules as to the depth of bath water which was indicated by a mark of bright red nail varnish on the inside of the bath, just four inches up from the base. There was a Mess with a gramophone, a library with books which they could borrow, a large kitchen, a ballroom and an attic. Though there were many chimneys, a Tudor statement of grandeur, there were few fires and it did not take the Simpson girls long to realise the lack of heating was due to no fires in the grates. That night they took to their bunks wearing Bobbie's Mam's woolly hats, socks and mittens, snuggled under the extra layer of Aunt Jayne's multi coloured crochet blankets and were introduced to the advantages of lemonade bottles filled with hot water.

The following morning the Simpson girls woke to that familiar smell of freshly baked bread and the unfamiliar sound of a charabanc outside. Rushing to the window they wiped away the mist from the inside of the leaded glass, and looking down saw the night-watch disembark from their transport and form a guard of honour on the drive as the good ship 'HMS Trepidation' pulled away from the front of the house to the sound of three hearty cheers and an array of Wrens' hats being thrown into the air. That indeed, was the start of a good day.

Later that day Mr Jones arrived at the Grange on a horse drawn cart with the girls' trunk, suitcase, bicycles and a bulky parcel wrapped in brown paper tied up with lots of rough string secured with sealing wax. Bobbie's Dad had finally got all the parts to finish her Christmas present and had carefully boxed, wrapped and sealed it for its long journey south. Luckily it had arrived at the Jones' cottage the very morning that Mr Jones had arranged to transport the rest of the girls' belongings to Tickford Farm and onwards to North Crawley.

Charlie and Bobbie were delighted to see Mr Jones and like everyone else, he too was eager to see what was in Bobbie's parcel.

As Bobbie cut through the rough string, pulled back the layers of brown paper and opened the box that familiar smell of Wrights Coal Tar antiseptic soap filled the room. Carefully removing the crunched up newspaper packaging Bobbie let out a shriek of delight as she lifted the custom built radio set from the soap box. Taking the radio straight into the Mess she plugged it in to the mains and turning the Bakelite knob began to tune it in. Little did she or her father know how well received his present would prove to be.

After saying goodbye to Mr Jones and agreeing to visit very soon, the Simpson girls decided to get to know the village.

Donning their woolly hats, mittens and scarves they got on to their bicycles, and like children with their rediscovered toys, took to the lanes of North Crawley and the freedom of the Buckinghamshire countryside.

{ 11 }

Broadened Horizons

LIFE AT THE GRANGE WAS CERTAINLY DIFFERENT. The journey to and from Bletchley Park was much longer and once back at the Grange the Wrens tended to make their own entertainment. The villagers were very welcoming and some Wrens joined St Firmin's Church choir, whilst others were introduced to the delights of gin and tonic in the Cock or the Chequers public houses. Those with bicycles wobbled in crocodile fashion through the winding country lanes to nearby Cranfield, Olney and Newport Pagnell, avoiding the deep road-side ditches and the odd cow which could prove challenging, especially on a dark night when the bikes at the front and the back shared the only set of lights. However, it would be the proximity to airfields, which for some would provide the best entertainment, and for many at the Grange the mixed emotions of the Moonlight Serenade.

It was on the night of Tuesday the 20th April 1943 when the Simpson girls were first introduced to the real Moonlight Serenade.

The night-watch transport did not come up to the house to collect the Wrens so they all had to walk down the end of the drive and pick up the charabanc by the Lodge in Pound Lane. On this clear and crisp night there had been no need for Bobbie to take her Dad's big Bakelite torch as the full moon lit their path below. Joining the other Wrens waiting at the end of the lane they heard the drone of aircraft engines and looking up saw the silhouettes of the majestic aircraft sailing across the cloudless night sky. In silent respect the girls stood to attention and one of the Wrens lifted her hand to her mouth and blew a kiss to the skies and, as if in response, the pilots tipped his aircraft's wings as it flew over the Grange.

In their first weeks at the Grange the Simpson girls had become used to the little Lysanders and Mosquitoes flitting cheekily overhead, watching them as they scurried across the day-time skies and sometimes hearing them venture out alone at night.

But there was something strangely different about these majestic birds hauling their great weight and secret cargos across the clear night skies of a full moon.

Like the rest of the villagers and other Wrens, the Simpson girls would get to know the moon periods, recognise the drone of the aircraft and pray that they and their crews would all return safely.

The flat lands of Buckinghamshire, Bedfordshire and Northamptonshire were ideal airfield country and there was no shortage of Allied aircrews ready, able and certainly more than willing to entertain the Wrens nesting in the Grange close to the edge of those counties' borders.

Soon after Charlie and Bobbie had arrived at the Grange one of the regular Cranfield Airfield dance invitations was posted on the letter board. The Simpson girls had just come off their night-watch and were sitting by the kitchen fire toasting thick slices of bread when Charlie turned to Bobbie and said, "Shall we go?"

"Go where?" asked Bobbie.

"To the Cranfield dance of course," replied Charlie.

"I'm not sure pet. You go."

"Come on. I am not going without you. You will enjoy it."

"No, you know me and crowds pet."

"I will look after you."

"You always do," smiled Bobbie.

"We look after each other," replied Charlie firmly.

Then, after a short silence Bobbie sat back in her chair and with the sense of fait accompli said, "Anyway pet, I don't have anything decent to wear."

"Oh yes you do," said Charlie triumphantly. "You cannot use that excuse. Come on, finish your toast."

Then taking Bobbie firmly by the hand she led her friend from the kitchen into the hall, up the stairs and back to their cabin.

Throwing open the lid of her old school trunk, which she had stowed in the corner of the cabin, Charlie lifted out the four dress boxes her mother had neatly packed at Christmas. Carefully folding back the tissue paper she took each dress out and laid them on her bunk; stood back and said, "Choose."

"Pardon?" said Bobbie.

"Choose a dress," prompted Charlie, "Which one would you like?"

"Oh, I can't," protested Bobbie.

"Oh yes you can," and picking up a floral print Charlie held it against Bobbie and asked, "This one?"

"It's ever so pretty," replied Bobbie.

"Right it is yours. Here you are," said Charlie handing the dress to Bobbie, "And this one? Do you like this one?" pointing to the more formal deep blue plain silk, "It brings out the blue in your eyes."

"Well yes." replied Bobbie, who for once was lost for words.

"Good. That's yours too."

"And here," said Charlie pulling some of the underwear and two boxes of nylon stockings out of the trunk and placing them on the bunk. "All yours."

Bobbie stood for a while looking across at Charlie then, gesturing towards the clothes on the bunk shook her head and said, "Sorry pet, I can't possibly accept these."

"Why on earth not Bobbie?" Charlie spelled out in a somewhat curt manner, "I accepted your Mam's mittens, hats, and scarves. Not to mention your Aunt Jayne's crochet blanket and the use of your Dad's radio set. All of which, may I say, have been a total godsend to me and gratefully received. So why can't you accept my gifts?"

"That's different pet, these are... well... just too much," Bobbie stammered.

In despair Charlotte snapped, "Nonsense. Absolute bloody nonsense Bobbie and you know it!" and not apologising for her language continued, "Sharing woolly hats, mittens, blankets, silk frocks and nylons. What is the difference?"

Shocked, not so much by her friend's generosity, but by her forcefulness and knowing she could not argue with Charlie's logic, Bobbie simply replied, "What can I say?"

In a soft tone of triumph Charlie smiled and putting her head on one side, and with a twinkle in her eyes winked and asked, "That you will come to the dance?"

"Well pet, I suppose it does."

Both girls laughed.

On the afternoon of the dance the girls met up outside Hut 11 and rushed to get their transport back to the Grange. Pleased to see Gladys at the helm of 'HMS Trepidation' they knew they were in safe hands as she steered her charges through the country lanes to North Crawley in good time to get ready for the Cranfield dance.

Back in their quarters the Simpson girls took a nail varnish depth bath and returned to their cabin to experiment with the shades of makeup that Charlie's mother had sent down that Christmas. They styled each other's hair; they delighted in the opulence of silk as they slipped on the underwear and felt its coolness against their skin; they rolled on the fully fashioned stockings, careful not to snag them and turned their legs to check their seams before stepping into their silk print dresses and uttering ... "Shoes!"

Charlie's mother had thought of everything, apart from court shoes. Thinking on her stocking feet Bobbie rushed into the next cabin where the girls were stirring to go down to the Mess before getting ready for their night-watch. Within minutes she returned in triumph carrying two pairs of court shoes.

"Bobbie. You are an Angel. How on earth did you do that?" said Charlie.

"Negotiation pet," replied Bobbie then admitted, "Though we have to give up our bikes for a week."

The Simpson girls slipped on the court shoes, gained two inches in height and shapely legs in the process and for a fleeting moment looked at each other in amazement.

"Roberta, you are so pretty," said Charlie.

"Charlotte, you don't look too bad yourself pet," replied Bobbie.

Charlie and Bobbie came down the grand Elizabethan staircase at Crawley Grange and into the main hall to join the rest of the Wrens as they awaited their transport to ferry them all over to Cranfield.

Wearing their new dresses and borrowed shoes, and in that fairy tale which shielded them from the stark realities of war, the Simpson girls went the ball.

{ 12 }

Old Friends and New

Crossed Wires

A S SPRING ARRIVED SO DID THE AMERICANS, Admiral Nelson and William. America had declared war on Germany in December 1941 and had later sent some of their code-breakers over to Bletchley Park to join forces with their British counterparts working in Huts 3 and 6. However, it wasn't until May 1943 that Bobbie had been introduced to Chuck. Considered to be one of Bletchley Park's more experienced Bombe operators,

Old Friends and New

Bobbie had been asked to explain the day to day running of the machines to him, and they had both become firm friends. Chuck had watched as Bobbie tested the machines and he had listened intently as she trained other Wrens to operate them. He had been amazed at Bobbie's patience and how carefully and systematically she plugged up the twelve miles of plaited wires. He had asked questions, made notes and sat next to her marvelling at her dexterity, skilfully identifying faults and using her eyebrow tweezers to tease the thin wires of the drums making minor repairs in order to get the job done, rather than wait for the RAF maintenance crews.

It was one spring day as the sun shone and the Wrens inside Hut 11a worked under the electric light that Chuck approached Bobbie and asked, "Bobbie, would you consider working in Washington?"

Bobbie looked up from her soldering, smiled and said, "Yes pet that would be canny. I could visit me Mam."

"Your Mom lives in Washington?" Chuck looked pleasantly surprised.

"No, West Cornforth actually," replied Bobbie still concentrating on the fine wires.

"Where's that?" asked Chuck.

Bobbie looked up at Chuck as if he should know better and replied, "About 20 miles north of Washington, she was born there."

"Where?" questioned Chuck.

Wishing to carry on with her work and getting slightly irritated by Chuck's questions Bobbie replied, "Washington!"

"Oh, your Mom's American?"

Firmly putting down her soldering iron and looking straight at Chuck she replied, "No, she's a Geordie. She's never set foot outside of England in her life."

Chuck looked puzzled, then shaking his head, smiled and drawled, "We're not talking about the same Washington are we? I'm talking about Washington D.C. "

Realizing that they had quite literally got their wires crossed, Bobbie turned to Chuck and with the confidence that only knowledge can bring, she calmly replied, "So am I pet, Washington D.C., as in Washington Durham County," and with an impish smile and the lift of her eye-brow asked, "Why? Is there any other?"

They both laughed, then giving her new found friend an Anglo-American history lesson and insight into the family tree of a certain George Washington, Bobbie returned to her soldering and thought no more of their conversation. There were indeed more pressing issues to attend to aboard HMS Pembroke V.

Since moving into Hut 11a, tucked behind the Stable Yard's cottage gardens, spring brought the welcome sound of children playing. The Budd family were the only ones living in Bletchley Park and the sound of the twin girls, Faye and Jean and their younger brother Neville playing happily together in the garden, heightened Bobbie's day. Secretly she looked forward to their long summer holidays and the welcome sound of children's laughter drifting over the Park.

However, it was during one night-watch, when the Budd children were safely tucked up in their beds, that the eerie sound of a cat fight brought Bobbie and her Dad's Bakelite torch up the side of Hut 11a and to the back of the Budd's garden.

Shining the torch on the battlefield of scrub Bobbie picked out the glint of an eye. Bending down she found a young cat with blood on its face looking helplessly up at her through its one remaining eye. Overcoming her fear of blood Bobbie instinctively bent down and picked it up. Even though the cat was frightened he had no energy to resist her as she cupped him in her arms and took him into the safety of the hut. After bathing his injured eye, and having had a short discussion with the rest of the night-watch, it was unanimously agreed that there was no reason under Navy rules why the cat should not stay. Every ship had its cat and he could be theirs. So it was on that spring night in 1943 that Admiral Nelson joined HMS Pembroke V.

It took some weeks to nurse the Admiral back to health. He spent much of his time cosseted and curled up in a box under one of the checking machines in Hut 11a. His eye was healing well, though Bobbie was worried he was still very thin. It was then that she had an idea. One evening, as the girls were sitting on board 'HMS Trepidation' making their way through Simpson and back to the Grange, Bobbie turned to her friend and asked, "Charlie, what's caviar?"

"Disgusting."

"No pet, I don't want to know what it tastes like. I want to know what it is."

"Oh, it is fish eggs," replied Charlie.

"I thought so. Can I have some?"

Charlie gave her friend a sideward glance and frowned, "Why? It is horrible," then with an apologetic smile she continued, "Sorry Bobbie, yes of course you can. There should still be some in Mrs Jones' pantry. We can ask her next time we visit. You may need to have it on plain biscuits or toast."

"Oh, no pet. It's not for me. It's for the cat."

"What!" exclaimed Charlie, "You cannot give caviar to a cat!"

"Why not?" asked Bobbie, "Cats like fish."

"Why not? Because it is frightfully expensive, probably illegal and apart from that, my mother would be beside herself if she thought her black market caviar was being given to a cat. Let alone what Mrs Jones would say."

With her tongue in cheek smile and her characteristic lift of that eyebrow Bobbie turned to her friend, pursed her lips and questioned, "How about if an Admiral ate her caviar then?"

The two girls laughed.

So it was that Admiral Nelson made a full recovery and got a taste of the high life. Mrs Jones was pleased to empty her pantry of the stock of caviar, and Charlie's mother was delighted that her daughter had made the acquaintance of an Admiral who enjoyed good food.

Back at Bletchley Park, as the service personnel increased, so did the civilian contingency and Charlie's section in Hut 8 completed their move to their purpose built brick building. It was on a fresh spring morning just after the tea boat had come round and the Wrens were standing by the window enjoying their tea break, that Charlie spotted a familiar figure.

Putting her tin mug down, she quickly ran outside.

"William?" she shouted.

The young man turned around.

"Charlie. What are you doing here?"

"I work here. More to the point what are you doing here?" asked Charlie.

"I work here too," replied William.

"Where?" asked Charlie, then immediately swallowed her words. "Sorry, forget I ever said that."

William smiled, "Let's just say, I come and go."

The two young people laughed and exchanged pleasantries before Charlie looked at her watch and exclaimed, "Gosh William, I must be off. It was so nice to see you."

"And you Charlie. Take care. Hope we will meet again soon," William replied and made his way up towards the Mansion as Charlie returned to her desk.

It was on the night of the 19th May 1943, as the two girls lay in their bunks listening for the sounds of the aircraft trawling across the moonlit sky that Charlie spoke to Bobbie about William for the very first time.

"Bobbie," prompted Charlie, "Are you still awake?"

"Yes pet," Bobbie replied a little dozily.

"Have I mentioned William to you?" Charlie continued.

"No, I don't think you have," yawned Bobbie.

"My mother introduced me to him at her Christmas cocktail party. He was the one who drove me back to Simpson on New Year's Eve. Did I not tell you?"

Bobbie tried to gather her thoughts and, as if replying to the ceiling of their cabin said, "You did tell us you'd had a lift back to the Jones' because your Mam thought your trunk was too heavy. But you didn't tell us who it was that drove you back."

"Well it was William," replied Charlie, "He was rather dishy. My mother was trying to make a match."

This caught Bobbie's attention and she hooked the top half of her body over her bunk and looking down at her friend below said, "You certainly didn't tell us that pet!"

"Well," replied Charlie pleased to have gained Bobbie's full attention, "I did not see him again, until today."

"Where?" Bobbie asked.

"Here."

"What? Here at the Grange?"

"No silly, there. There at the Park. He was walking past my window."

"You're kiddin' us!" replied Bobbie, now fully awake and in need of more information.

"I am most definitely not kiddin' you," mimicked Charlie, "It is perfectly true," and continued, "The tea boat had just arrived and I was standing looking out over the lake and drinking my tea when I saw William walk by. I was so shocked I just put my mug down and ran."

"What was he doing there?" asked Bobbie.

"Oh, really Bobbie, you know better than to ask me that!" teased Charlie.

"You know what I meant pet," said Bobbie as she shifted back in her bunk.

"Of course I do," smiled Charlie, "in fact I made the mistake of asking him where he worked, before I ate my words. It is so easily done. Sometimes I think it is far better not to say anything at all, even if you seem so terribly rude," replied Charlie.

"I know pet. It's hard sometimes when you worry if you have made a mistake and you can't tell anyone," Bobbie said, looking into the distance.

"Why? Have you made a terrible mistake Bobbie?" Charlie asked in a worried tone.

"Oh no not me, well not one I know of, but I think one of the other girls on our watch must have. She just kept bursting into tears for no reason. No one seemed to know what was wrong with her so they took her off to the sick bay and we haven't seen her since. She didn't have the chance to say goodbye."

Charlie looked up at the base of the bunk bed above her and said, "That's awful. I know we have to keep secrets, but whatever happens we will always say goodbye. Won't we?"

"Of course we will pet, always," reassured Bobbie.

The two girls lay for a while before Bobbie broke the silence and said, "Well pet, tell us about William? Are you going to see him again?"

"I'm not sure. It would be nice," said Charlie as she rolled over and pulled her blankets up around her ears.

As the Simpson girls lay safely in their bunks in Crawley Grange they heard the drone of the Moonlight Serenade making its way across the clear night sky carrying its secret cargos across the English countryside and onwards to war, and they prayed for its safe return.

Spring turned to summer and brought a few surprises. Admiral Nelson had found his sea legs and ventured out making friends and playing with the Budd twins in their garden. Bobbie was pleased to see the Admiral was finally putting on weight and seemed much more contented and far more confident, sometimes staying out late, though always making sure to be back in Hut 11a before curfew. However, one July evening the Admiral did not return and went absent without leave. A search party was sent out the following morning and Bobbie had even peeped over the Budd's garden fence to ask the children if they had seen him. Everyone knew cats were independent and they had thought that he had probably gone off to find a new home. Bobbie was not so sure, and though the Admiral was thoroughly spoiled by all the Wrens in Hut 11a, he had a certain fondness for Bobbie which was reciprocated, and she knew he would not have gone far.

So, when the time came, it was to Bobbie that the Admiral introduced her kittens. In their rush to give the one eyed cat a name none of the Wrens had even given a thought to check its gender. Admiral Nelson proved to be a good and caring mother rearing her four healthy kittens all of which, thanks to Bobbie, were found good homes at Bletchley and Crawley Grange.

{ 13 }

Unspoken Words

I N THE AUGUST OF 1943, just twelve months after being drafted to HMS Pembroke V, both Simpson girls had demonstrated their skills and were suitably rewarded with responsibility and promotion through the ranks to Petty Officers. As expected of any of her ratings their First Officer was pleased that the girls did not allow their promotion to go to their heads; apart from their delight in wearing the tricorn which Charlie had commented gave so much scope for a more flattering hairstyle and Bobbie thought was ideal to cover up a multitude of sins. Their promotion did, however, give the Simpson girls an excuse to celebrate, and it was to the Jones' that they took Charlie's mother's picnic basket and the food hamper.

Since leaving Simpson the two girls had visited Mr and Mrs Jones regularly. On their days off they had cycled over to Simpson or hitched a lift often staying the night in the comfort of their own beds which Mrs Jones kept aired for them, just in case.

When returning to North Crawley after a long night-watch, they had arranged with Gladys to steer 'HMS Trepidation' slowly past the church so that they could wave to Mrs Jones who would be waiting at her front door.

Charlie had continued to share the bounty of her mother's food parcels with the Jones' and when Mr Jones' wireless set needed to go in for repair the two girls carted Bobbie's radio from the Grange over to Simpson, so that Mr Jones could keep up with current affairs.

So it was, on an August evening four unlikely friends sat under the shade of the apple trees at the top of the Jones' garden. The red check picnic cloth covered the bare wooden table and the four napkins were neatly rolled in their rings next to the plates. The cutlery was polished and the champagne flutes filled with home-made ginger beer, and a bounty of sandwiches, fruit and scones lay on the table.

In that late evening the leisurely clip-clop of the horse's hooves could be heard on the tow path as it pulled the barge making its way along the canal to its moorings for the night and a well earned rest. As the friends ate and chatted, the fragrance of jasmine filled the air; skylarks glided silently across the sky and a lone robin serenaded them from the safety of the honeysuckle bush. In this peaceful place, war seemed so far away and the girls needed little persuasion to stay the night.

The morning after the picnic in the Jones' garden the Simpson girls left the comfort of their soft beds and got ready for the day-watch. Mrs Jones had prepared breakfast and, instead of going straight out into the garden she had stayed in the kitchen where Mr Jones had asked the girls if he could take a photograph of them in their new hats. They readily agreed and dusting themselves down, straightening their uniform and checking their new tricorns, they went out into the garden, linked arms and looked directly into the lens of the Box Brownie camera and smiled.

With their photographs taken they returned to the kitchen and Mrs Jones. In the privacy of her own home and, as if she knew something they did not, the old lady took each one of the girls in her arms and hugged them tight before walking down with them to St Thomas' Church to wait for their transport and to wave them goodbye.

Unspoken Words

Since the code-breakers of Bletchley Park had become aware of the addition of a fourth wheel on the German Naval Enigma machines, work had been started with the Americans to develop a Bombe machine which would speed up the process of breaking into those Enigma messages. Though the three wheel Bombs could be used, the process was quite lengthy and Chuck had learned a lot from Bobbie about the workings of those original machines.

It was on a day early in September 1943 that Chuck was working with Bobbie in Hut 11a. He knew that they were testing the machine working on a four wheel German Naval Enigma message, and at each stop of the machine Chuck began to get more and more excited. Then, when it seemed all the letters on the Menu linked and had been checked he stood next to Bobbie eagerly waiting the response as she lifted the telephone receiver to call the findings through. As Wren in Charge, it was Bobbie's job to confirm those findings and wait for further instructions. Dialling the extension she listened for the tone and waited for the telephone to be answered.

The telephone on Charlie's desk rang out. Automatically picking up the receiver she answered accordingly and was met with silence at the other end, followed by a familiar voice, "Charlie? Is that you?"

Then the line went dead as both girls simultaneously slammed their receivers down and looked accusingly at the telephones in front of them. Both girls had signed the Official Secrets Act and were duty bound never to talk about the work they did, not even with their family nor friends, including fellow Wrens. Neither Charlie nor Bobbie had ever spoken to each other about their work aboard HMS Pembroke V and to hear the sound of each other's voices on the other end of the telephone line came as a shock.

"Bobbie," asked Chuck, "are you OK? You look as if you've seen a ghost, or heard one."

Taking a deep breath and quickly pulling herself together she replied, "I'm OK, pet" and lifting the telephone receiver redialled the number, this time more prepared for the familiar voice at the other end as she waited for her friend Charlie to answer.

In her cabin Charlie picked up the receiver once again and responded to the findings and the request coming from the other end of the line. Within a matter of time she herself was making a call back to Bobbie to confirm that the job was up. Neither of the girls acknowledged recognition of each other and they both maintained the strictest protocols. Not another word was spoken, nor the matter ever mentioned.

Though there was the usual measured elation in Hut 11a at a job done Bobbie wondered why Chuck was so excited. She put it down to the fact he was an American and thought no more of it as she stripped down the machine and set it up in readiness to tackle yet another Menu and another network's messages.

Unbeknown to Bobbie, over in Naval Decrypts Charlie had turned that message from a string of meaningless letters into plain German text and sent it through to Naval Intelligence for translation and out into the theatre of war. From their moorings in the purpose built brick buildings of HMS Pembroke V in the Buckinghamshire countryside neither Bobbie nor Charlie would ever know the part they played in the eventual capture of the *U-617*, the very U-boat which had sent the *M. V. Athelsultan* to the bottom of the Atlantic Ocean the previous September.

So it was, in the early hours of the 12th September 1943, *Wellingtons* '*P*' and '*J*' of *179 Squadron* attacked the *U-617* whilst in waters off the North African coast and brought the German *U-617's* nineteen month reign of terror to an end.

October 1943

Since joining HMS Pembroke V in the summer of 1942 both Simpson girls had been inseparable, apart from their Christmas leave. Due to the length of the journey back up to Durham, Bobbie had not been home since, and Charlie who was used to spending time at boarding school, had only visited her parents in London once. So with a week's leave approaching both girls decided to go down to London. Charlie had said that they could stay with her parents or find somewhere else for a few nights and hopefully Charlie could arrange to introduce Bobbie to William.

They had made their plans and on the day before going on their well earned leave the girls disembarked from 'HMS Trepidation' to take up their stations. They agreed to meet at the end of their watch at 1600 hours outside Hut 11 as usual and go back to the Grange to get a good night's sleep. Their bags were packed in readiness and they would catch the early morning transport the following day to Bletchley Station and their train to London.

However, no sooner had Bobbie arrived at her post in Hut 11a than she was summoned to the Mansion and an escort was sent to collect her. She had never been inside the Mansion before and thoughts ran through her mind that she had forgotten something or more to the point, said something out of turn. Then the realisation of that telephone call came to mind. Surely she had done nothing wrong. Neither she nor Charlie mentioned it to each other, nor had she told anyone else about it, not even Chuck when he had asked if she was OK.

Walking by the tennis courts and across to the front of the Mansion, Bobbie was taken into the large Entrance Hall and up the heavily polished carved staircase to an equally grand first floor landing and on into one of the rooms at the front of the house. There was a bare light bulb above the door and as she entered the room her escort left, closed the door firmly behind her and the light was switched on, a sign that in no event were they to be disturbed.

Bobbie nervously faced her First Officer and a civilian she had never met before. As a minor rank Bobbie saluted the First Officer, who reciprocated and asked her to take a seat. She was formally reminded that she had signed the Official Secrets Act and of the importance of the work she was doing, particularly with the Americans on the developments of the new Bombe machines. Quietly panicking she thought that it must be something to do with that telephone call with Charlie, or it may be Chuck. If she was facing disciplinary action, why was a civilian involved and why had she been invited to sit down? Very soon everything became clear. Pulling her attention back to what was being said to her she realised she was not being disciplined; she was in fact being drafted to Washington D.C. in the United States of America. Bobbie was shell shocked as she listened in complete silence.

Her work and expertise with the Bombe had been noted and she was told that she was second only to one where working the machines were concerned. She would travel up to *Gourock* in Scotland that afternoon and once there she would report to the ship's captain, Captain Illingsworth. She would be accommodated on board prior to it setting sail on 18th October. Once the ship sailed she was to travel in civilian clothes until she reached America, though she would continue to receive her orders through Captain Illingsworth until the ship docked in New York. She would not travel across the Atlantic alone, she would be accompanied by Lieutenant Charles Hurst of the United States Navy, whom she knew; and she would continue her journey to Washington with him, where she would receive further orders.

Not that they needed to explain but Bobbie was told that Leading Wren Doreen Smith had been the original selection. However, she had been taken ill, hence the short notice. All the necessary paperwork had been taken care of and a driver would take Bobbie straight over to her quarters to collect her kit. She was not to tell anyone where she was going, nor what she was doing and could only write to her family and friends once she had arrived in America. She was told her driver was waiting outside and she was handed her orders, papers and travel warrants.

The shock tactics had worked and Bobbie had responded to her orders as a professional member of the Royal Navy; though she could feel the mixed emotions of relief at not being disciplined, and panic as to the suddenness of her move. The tears welled up inside as she took her orders, dutifully saluted and turned to leave.

As if reading her mind the First Officer said, "Don't worry we will tell Petty Officer Charlotte Bingham that you have been drafted. You can write to her once you arrive in New York."

Bobbie nodded, unable to say a word in case a sea of tears erupted.

Waiting outside the door Bobbie was pleased to see a friendly face as Gladys introduced herself as Bobbie's driver. The two girls walked out of the Mansion to the car parked right outside. Gladys opened the rear door, and Bobbie slipped into the back seat. She did not utter a word as Gladys retraced Bobbie's steps out of Bletchley Park, under the railway bridge and along through to Fenny Stratford, over the level crossing, down the lane in to Simpson village, taking the bend by the Plough and on towards St Thomas' Church. It was when she passed the Jones' cottage and caught a glimpse of Mrs Jones by her front door that a tear fell from Bobbie's eye.

As the car pulled up outside Crawley Grange, Gladys waited whilst Bobbie went in through the main door and up the grand staircase. Opening the cabin door she looked around at the kit bags, Charlie's trunk and her own suitcase, all packed for their leave in London. She sat down on Charlie's bunk and wondered how she could tell her friend what she was doing without disobeying orders. Then reaching into her shoulder bag she pulled out the letter she had carried with her since that fateful September morning in 1942, and folding it back to reveal her Ma's words laid it on Charlie's pillow.

"Some people come into our lives and quickly go, others stay a while and leave footprints on our hearts and we are never ever the same."

Picking up her kit bag and suitcase, she hooked her Aunt Jayne's blanket over her arm and leaving the cabin for the very last time, went down the stairs. In the shadows of the grand Tudor hall Chief Petty Officer Lillian Ashley stood in silence and gently stroking the young cat, watched as Bobbie closed the front door behind her and got into the waiting car.

Later that afternoon the Glasgow train pulled out of Bletchley Station and Bobbie began her long journey north. Taking her seat by the window she watched as the Buckinghamshire countryside gave way to war torn towns and cities of the Midlands and Northwest of England. As the autumn sun dropped in the sky she caught a glimpse of her reflection in the train's window and saw the images of some of those who had, for whatever moment in time, left footprints on her heart. She saw her Parents and Grand-parents, her Aunt Edith, her Aunt Jayne and her Cousin Peter, Mr Heppell and Mr Blenkinsop, Mr and Mrs Jones, the Budd twins, Doreen and Admiral Nelson and, as Bobbie slowly pulled down the blind she closed her tear filled eyes and registered the final image of her good friend Charlie.

Back on board HMS Pembroke V Charlie had been called to the Mansion and been told of Bobbie's draft and later that day she had travelled back to the Grange aboard 'HMS Trepidation' with Gladys at the wheel. As if trying to tell her something, Gladys turned to Charlie as she got out of the charabanc and said, "Goodbye pet."

Charlie smiled, thanked Gladys and followed behind the rest of her watch towards the house to prepare to go home on leave alone. Then suddenly turning on her heel Charlie called out, "Gladys! Are you going straight back to Bletchley?"

"Yes," replied Gladys.

"Good. May I hitch a lift to the Railway Station?"

"Of course," said Gladys.

"I will get my bags. I won't be a moment."

Rushing up the stairs Charlie opened the cabin door as the draught sent the letter floating to the floor. Reaching for her bags she took one last look around the room before noticing the piece of paper on the floor. Picking it up she read the verse, and in a world of secrecy, codes and ciphers she instinctively knew what her friend was trying to say. Folding the letter, she put it in her hand bag, left the cabin and made her way back to the charabanc and Bletchley Railway Station.

Charlie thanked Gladys for the lift and telephoned her mother from the public phone box to say that she would make her own way over to her parents' flat that evening before deciding what she would do for the rest of her leave.

Sitting by the window on the London bound train she looked out into the darkness of the late evening and carefully pulling down the blind remembered all those friends that, if it had not been for war and the melting pot which was HMS Pembroke V, she would never have had the privilege to meet. Taking Bobbie's letter from her bag she re-read the short verse and closing her eyes thought of the fun, laughter, tears and the pain and felt Bobbie's footprint firmly on her heart.

So it was, some days later on a cold October night in 1943, as Bobbie lay sleeping in her cabin and her ship sailed out of safe home waters to cross the Atlantic Ocean, her friend Charlie made her way across London to meet William. It was then that the German missile hit its target and dealt its fatal blow.

{ 14 }

Sunset

21st December 2011

THE VETERAN'S WORDS HAD BOUNCED OFF THE BRICK WALLS, the cement floor and around the redundant space which was now Hut 11. With a sudden jerk Susan was brought firmly back into the twenty-first century as the old lady gently whispered, "You see my dear, like so many others, there was just no time to say goodbye."

Then, as if aware of something Susan was not, the old lady stood up, smiled and looking down at Susan said, "Goodbye my dear. Thank you so much for listening to me. It is time for me to go now."

Susan instinctively got to her feet to accompany the old lady out of the building when the lady turned to her, smiled, tilted her head to one side, lifted one eyebrow and nodding towards the table said, "Don't forget your gloves pet."

Thanking the lady for reminding her, Susan walked over to the table to collect her gloves and heard the sound of the door of Hut 11 open behind her. Automatically looking over her shoulder, expecting to see the lady making her way out, she was shocked to see the room empty, save for Tony's silhouette framed in the doorway.

"Oh Tony, you made me jump," gasped Susan.

"Sorry," he said, "Is it OK if I lock up now?"

"Yes, yes of course. I just came back for my gloves."

"Not again!" he smiled, "You should have them pinned to your sleeves."

They both laughed and making her way to the door Susan instinctively looked up at the clock. It had stopped at 3.55pm. She checked the time on her mother's watch. It was five minutes to four. Susan looked puzzled.

"Something wrong?" asked Tony.

"I think the clock may have stopped."

"No problem," replied Tony, "I'll pop a new battery in it tomorrow."

Susan smiled and wondered why her watch had also stopped at the same time. Then making her way out of the building she turned to Tony and asked, "Did you see two old ladies outside just now?"

Firmly locking the doors and checking the handle Tony looked back at Susan and shaking his head said, "No. There's no one about. All the visitors have gone home."

"Are you sure?" asked Susan, "I was just talking to a veteran in here who was meeting her friend outside."

With that cheeky grin which lit up his whole face, he winked and said, "Been at the Christmas spirit already then?"

Susan enjoyed the banter on the Park and taking no offence replied, "Ah, you noticed."

As Tony left Hut 11 to make his way up to check the other buildings, they wished each other a Happy Christmas and Susan walked back across the tennis courts to her car, just as the snow began to fall. Looking over the Park for the old lady and her friend Susan was comforted to see two figures, arm in arm making their way down towards the lake. Lifting her hand she waved and said, "Goodbye."

Reaching the car she opened the doors and taking off her fur and coat she neatly placed them on the back seat. Settling into the driver's seat she turned the key in the ignition and switched on the headlights. As she did so, the beam of light picked up the glint of an eye and the dark figure of a cat rose nobly to its feet, stood a while and then gracefully turned before disappearing into the shrub of the Stable Yard's cottage gardens.

Manoeuvring the car from its parking space, Susan checked in her rear view mirror. The snow was falling fast and the mirror framed an image of the Victorian Mansion covered in a blanket of snow, which in turn concealed the footprints of the day. Tilting the mirror she looked straight back at her own reflection, smiled, winked and thought. It had, indeed, been a most interesting day.

With the Christmas celebrations over Susan sat at the breakfast table drinking tea and eating Marmite toast soldiers. Jim was already at his desk in the study making full use of the latest communication technology. Opening the case of her brand new Kindle, Susan switched it on. The little dog, knowing her every move, snuggled his head against her fluffy Christmas slippers and settled down for an early morning doze.

Susan had been very strict and had not opened any e-mails over the holiday period so, as she accessed her mail-box the messages came in thick and fast. Quickly glancing through the spam she highlighted them and deleted them with one press of a key, then returning to the in-box spotted a subject line that all those connected with Bletchley Park dreaded... "Sad News"

Opening the e-mail Susan did not recognise the lady's name and as she followed the link to the Times obituary page she was prepared for the usual headline, 'Bletchley Park Code-breaker dies...' She was, however, ill prepared for the face that looked straight back at her from the screen. Just like the time they had met in Hut 11, Susan's heart leapt into her throat.

OBITUARY

Lady Roberta Ambrose

Lady Roberta Ambrose (nee Newton) died at her home on Wednesday 21st December 2011. Known as Bobbie Newton during the Second World War, Lady Ambrose served with the Women's Royal Naval Service (Wrens) as a Bombe operator at Bletchley Park between August 1942 and October 1943.

During the Second World War, Bletchley Park was the secret base of the Government Code & Cypher School (GC&CS) where enemy ciphered messages, including those generated through the Enigma machines were decrypted. It was the job of the Bombe operators to work the machines which assisted in identifying the settings used in those ciphered messages.

On her arrival aboard HMS Pembroke V, the naval term used for Bletchley Park during those war years, Bobbie Newton shared a billet in the near-by village of Simpson with fellow Wren, Charlotte Bingham and it was during their time in the village that both girls became affectionately known as the Simpson girls.

In 1943 the Simpson girls moved to naval quarters in Crawley Grange situated in the village of North Crawley. The girls continued their work at Bletchley Park and maintained their vow of secrecy, not even confiding in each other about the work they did. Later that year both girls rose through the ranks to Petty Officer.

In October 1943 Petty Officer Roberta Newton was assigned to special duties and, on the 18th October 1943, she set sail across the Atlantic Ocean to New York aboard the Queen Mary. She was accompanied on that trip by Lieutenant

Footprints

Charles (Chuck) Hurst of the United States Navy who was assisting with the development of the four wheel Bombe machines

As Roberta was crossing the Atlantic Ocean her good friend Charlotte Bingham was killed, whilst on leave in London, during the German air raid of the 21st October 1943.

After the war Roberta Newton returned to England and was seconded to the Foreign Office in London where she met her future husband William Ambrose.

Roberta and William married in September 1947, by which time William had inherited his father's title. They have two children Peter and Charlotte.

It was not until sometime after the war that both Lord and Lady Ambrose, known as Bobbie and Bill to their friends, revealed that they had both worked at Bletchley Park during the Second World War.

A Durham miner's daughter, Lady Ambrose worked tirelessly to enable girls to follow their paths in engineering and technology and she was given an Honorary Degree by Durham University. She embraced all forms of technology and her work was followed by many.

Lady Ambrose was involved in many charities including the R.S.P.C.A and was patron of a local sanctuary for cats.

Daughter Charlotte said that both she and her mother should have visited Bletchley Park on the day of her mother's death. Unfortunately her mother had caught a chill and they had all decided it was better that she stayed at home.

Lady Ambrose died peacefully with her female cat called Admiral Nelson, cupped safely in her arms

Sunset

Bobbie's husband William posted a note on his wife's Obituary Guest Book which simply read,

"Goodnight my Angel"

An anonymous subscriber later posted...

"Some people come into our lives and quickly go, others stay a while and leave footprints on our hearts, and we are never, ever, the same.

{ End }

{ 15 }

Behind the Book

Whilst researching this book I have been privileged to interview and correspond with a number of people who lived and worked at Bletchley Park, and with others willing to share their war-time experiences outside of that place. Many people have given me access to private papers and I have been able to call on material stored in the Bletchley Park Archive, reports produced by English Heritage and other files in The National Archive at Kew.

This is the first in the series of historical novels which tells the story of life at Bletchley Park during the Second World War. By combining facts with memories, the fictional characters provide the reader with a vehicle in which to travel back in time to one of Britain's most secret establishments, the Government Code & Cypher School.

Behind The Book

I am often asked by visitors which books they should read. Book selection is very personal and there are many excellent publications including biographies and auto-biographies; books explaining the technical and mathematical work of men, women and machines, all of which provide an insight into the working of that place. However, there are few books which harness all aspects of life, both inside and outside of Bletchley Park and it is hoped, that this book does just that.

Footprints

Acknowledgements

I would like to thank fellow Bletchley Park volunteers and staff for their valuable assistance. To Clarence, Jean, Joyce, Margaret, and Tony for allowing me to use their real names

(In alphabetical order)

Jean Cheshire (nee Budd), Volunteer, for her childhood recollections of living at Bletchley Park during the Second World War.

John Gallehawk, Volunteer, for his confirmation of war-time history; and the workings of Bletchley Park. Additional documents regarding the capture of the U-617 and copies of the associated U-boat intercepted messages decrypted at Bletchley Park and stored in The National Archive in London.

Joel Greenberg, Volunteer, for confirmation of the Queen Mary's Atlantic crossings.

Katherine Lynch, Bletchley Park Media Manager, for providing the links to the appropriate Official Bletchley Park Podcasts regarding the 'purchase' of Bletchley Park by Admiral Sir Hugh Sinclair.

Bryan Mead, Volunteer, for sight of the Leon Estate's Sale Catalogue (1937); copies of property sale documents, and the Bletchley Park Estate Map (1937/8).

The late Dr Brian Oakley, Volunteer, for his extensive knowledge of Bletchley Park, its buildings and the locations of the sections within the Park.

Steve Ovens, Bletchley Park Archive, for the location of Land Registry documents with reference to the sale of Bletchley Park (1938).

John Pether, Volunteer, for the GPO National Trunk Cable Map.

Sue Pinder, Volunteer, for her photograph of Bletchley Park Mansion in the snow.

Cheryl Salmon, Volunteer, for her time proof reading.

Dave Steadman, Volunteer, for his knowledge of HMS Petard and the U559.

Joyce Sussex, Bletchley Park Customer Services, for her memories of war-time Bletchley and Fenny Stratford.

Dave White, Volunteer, for his explanations of war-time BBC radio communications and Station X.

Behind The Book

Bletchley Park Veterans

Mrs Ruth Bourne and Mrs Eva Knowhill for describing their lives as Wrens working on the Bombe machines.

Mrs Honor Grimes for her memories of her Atlantic Ocean crossing to Canada as an evacuee in 1940, and her return journey to Liverpool in 1943, and for the recollections of her recruitment to Bletchley Park as a civilian typist working on the modified Type-X machines.

The late Mrs Barbara Wyllie, Queen Alexandra's Royal Naval Nursing Sister in Charge of the Crawley Grange Sick Bay; and Mrs Eva Knowhill for their memories of living at Crawley Grange.

Rolf Noskwith for his modest appraisal of the code-breaking work he undertook in Hut 8.

The History of Bletchley Park

The history of Bletchley Park is based on the cumulative knowledge of Bletchley Park veterans and volunteers; the Official Bletchley Park Guided Tour and the Bletchley Park Archive. Additional material sourced and confirmed through English Heritage, The National Archive and a number of excellent publications.

Bletchley Park Transport Routes

Mrs Elaine Wright daughter of F.J. Gemmell who served at Bletchley Park in the Military Section SIXTA between 1941 and 1945.

Mrs Wright has provided a copy of her father's Ordnance Survey map of the period with the roads and routes identified by hand written numbers marked out in red pencil.

Ordnance Survey of England and Wales

Geographical Section, General Staff, No 3907

Published by the War Office, 1942.

Crawley Grange

Miranda Koss for inviting me to visit her family home in Crawley Grange to check the location of the rooms.

Atlantic Crossings

Sherborne Girls' School archive documents providing insight into the experiences of some of their girls and of other children evacuated to Canada who crossed the Atlantic Ocean on board the S.S. Duchess of Athol and the S.S. Duchess of Bedford.

M.V. Athelsultan

The late Mrs Winifred Shields for her personal story regarding the loss of her first husband Geoffrey Charlton, one of the two telegraphists on board the fated Merchant Vessel Athelsultan.

Additional Information, References and Books

This short guide, including publications and qualified web links may be of use to those readers wishing to learn more about Bletchley Park and other subjects mentioned in this novel.

Please note all links, locations and books were available at the time of publication.

Chapter 2 - Bletchley Park

The Victorian Mansion - details of the Leon Estate
"A Maudlin and Monstrous Pile: The Mansion at Bletchley Park", by Kathryn A Morrison, English Heritage
English Heritage Floor Plans of the Seckham and the extended Leon house.
Phase-plan of Bletchley Park 1878 to 1906 (Page 91 Figure 6)
Ground-floor plan of Bletchley Park Mansion (Page 98 Figure 12)
www.english-heritage.org.uk/content/imported-docs/pt/thehistoryofthemansionbletchleypark.pdf

A list of rooms and their uses between1878 and 1945 taken from a number of sources including the English Heritage document noted above.

Chapter 3 - A Secret Site - Government Code & Cypher School

Details of the Sale of the Leon Estate
Bletchley Park Sale Brochure dated the 28th July 1937
Knight, Frank and Rutley - Land Agents & Surveyors, London
Whatley, Hill & Co, Auctioneers and Estate Agents, London

Please Note: Lot 1 The Mansion and grounds did not reach its reserve in the auction of 1937 and was sold privately to a building consortium under Captain Hugh Falkner. Part of that Lot was later 'sold' to Admiral Hugh Sinclair.

"...for all intent and purposes the Mansion and some of its grounds became the property of Admiral Hugh Sinclair"

Behind The Book

Land Registry documents BM528; BM677 and P7624 13th June 1938 - Bletchley Park Trust.

Please Note: The GCHQ Historian confirms that, though Sinclair's name appears on the documents, Sinclair did not use his own money to purchase the property.

"Mythbusters" co-presented at Bletchley Park by Michael Smith on the 14th October 2012

audioboo.fm/Bletchleypark

Bletchley Park Podcast Extra 10th November 2012 S01E04

Bletchley Park Podcast Extra 17th November 2012 E10

Rail and Telecommunications Networks

Map of the London Midland and Scottish Railway Network of the period can be found at

en.wikipedia.org/wiki/London,_Midland_and_Scottish_Railway

General Post Office Communications and Repeater Stations

GPO National Trunk Cable Map of the period – John Pether.

A reproduction of this map can be found in the book

"Bletchley Park's Secret Sisters", by John Taylor.

(A review on this book can be found at www.booksonbletchleypark.co.uk)

Chapter 4 – Bletchley Park at War

A Walk in the Park

Details taken from the Official Bletchley Park Guided Tour.

Books written by Bletchley Park code-breakers include:-

"Code Breakers – The Inside Story of Bletchley Park", edited by F H Hinsley & Alan Stripp

"DILLY – The Man Who Broke Enigma", by Mavis Batey

"Enigma Variations – Love, War & Bletchley Park", by Irene Young

"The Bletchley Park Codebreakers", edited by Ralph Erskine & Michael Smith

Chapter 12 'Hut 8 From the Inside', written by Rolf Noskwith

(Reviews on these books can be found at

www.booksonbletchleypark.co.uk)

A number of veterans' recollections can be found on the Bletchley Park's Official Website

www.bletchleypark.org.uk/content/hist/history/RollofHonour.rhtm
www.bletchleypark.org.uk/content/hist/history/Veterans.rhtm

Pigeons
The "Pigeons in War" leaflet by The Royal Pigeon Association provides a brief overview of the work of homing pigeons during both World Wars. There is an exhibition currently on show at Bletchley Park.
www.bletchleypark.org.uk/content/visit/whattosee/pigions.rhtm

Further information can be found on The Royal Pigeon Racing Association website
www.rpra.org

Chapter 5 - The Journey

F.A.N.Y. Alnwick Unit
"Commander – Her Grace The Duchess of Northumberland founded this Unit in April 1941 in response to requests from the Northumberland Red Cross and the Air Ministry of Northumberland.... ....This Unit was disbanded in October 1945."
The National Archive - TNA HS7/7

The Driving Test
"Driving tests were suspended for the duration of the Second World War."
www.gov.uk/government/publications/history-of-road-safety-and-the-driving-test

Mr Heppell's Garage in Station Road, West Cornforth is no longer there.
Mr Blenkinsop's Bus and Coach Company, Scarlet Band based in Station Road continues to serve the local community in the North East of England
"Scarlet Band was established in 1921 by Sidney Blenkinsop and although we originally started as a taxi operator, we quickly moved into the commercial sector, running our first buses in 1925". Graeme Torrance of Scarlet Band
www.scarletbandbuses.co.uk/about.php

Chapter 6 - HMS Pembroke V

The Bombe Machine
John Harper and the Bombe Rebuild Team
www.jharper.demon.co.uk/bombe1.htm
www.bletchleypark.org.uk/content/visit/whattosee/BombeRebuildProject.rhtm

Chapter 7 -The Letter

M.V. Athelsultan
The details of the sinking of the M.V. Athelsultan is taken from the research undertaken by Mr. Eric P Smith and his correspondence with the late Mrs Winifred Shields

www.uboat.net/allies/merchants/ships/2202.html
Cullercoats Coastal Radio Station
www.coastalradio.org.uk/ukstations/cullercoats/cullercoats.html
Adelphi Hotel
"Brief History on the Adelphi Hotel" (article) and "The Story of a Great Undertaking" (booklet) provided by the Britannia Adelphi Hotel, Liverpool

City of Benares: www.uboat.net/allies/merchants/ships/532.html

German U-boat U-48: www.uboat.net/boats/u48.htm

Chapter 8 - Battle against Time

Battle of the Atlantic
As well as the other aspects of code breaking, the following book covers the battle to break into German U-boat Enigma in greater detail.
"ENIGMA – The Battle for the Code", by Hugh Sebag-Montefiore
(A review on this book can be found at www.booksonbletchleypark.co.uk)

HMS Petard and the U-559
Lieutenant Tony Fasson RN , Able Seaman Colin Grazier and Tommy Brown.
"The Real Enigma Heroes", by Phil Shanahan
(The Petard Exhibition can be seen at Bletchley Park – Dave Steadman)
www.uboat.net/allies/warships/ship/4495.html

Chapter 9 - Home on Leave

The Dorchester Hotel
British Prime Minister Winston Churchill, American General Dwight D Eisenhower
en.wikipedia.org/wiki/The_Dorchester
Claridge's Hotel
www.claridges.co.uk/about-the-hotel/history/

Chapter 10 - Sea of Change

The official account dated 18th February 1943 recording the increase in personnel; the use of outstations for the Bombe machines and the extra Wrens' quarters.

"The High Speed Machinery [Bombes] which test the "menus" prepared by Huts 6 and 8 are served by the W.R.N.S.   The machinery is now dispersed to Gayhust, Wavendon, Adstock and Stanmore" ...

"This station [Stanmore] will have some 750 W.R.N.S. and some 80 maintenance R.A.F. mechanics"...

"B.P.'s Hut 11a is now partly used for training, partly also for the experimental work as well as ordinary operations"...

TNA - HW14/67

Chapter 11 - Broadened Horizons

Life at Crawley Grange taken from interviews with Mrs Eva Knowhill and the late Mrs Barbara Wyllie

Chapter 12 - Old Friends and New

The Americans

"The Bletchley Park Codebreakers", edited by Ralph Erskine & Michael Smith.

'Most Helpful and Co-operative: GC&CS and the Development of American Diplomatic Cryptanalysis, 1941-2', written by David Alvarez.

Washington, Durham County

www.visionofbritain.org.uk/place/place_page.jsp?p_id=1214

Chapter 13 - Unspoken Words

Beaching / scuttling of the U-617

"The U617 was attached by Wellington 'P' and 'J' of 179 Squadron......At (0315 aircraft 'J' (P Off W.H. Brunini) arrived and delivered another six depth charges despite fierce flak which killed the aircraft's rear gunner...." (August-September 1943 page 145)

"U-Boats Lost", by Paul Kemp

U-617, Wellington P and Wellington J

179 Squadron - R.A.F. Station, North Front Gibraltar

12th September 1943

The National Archive - Operations Record Book - AIR27/1127 pages 13 to 15

Intercepted German messages dated 12th September 1943 decrypted at Bletchley Park – The National Archive

www.uboat.net/boats/u617.htm

Chapter 14 - Sunset

RMS Queen Mary – Record of Sailings 1943
Captain Illingsworth was one of Queen Mary's Captains who steered the liner across the Atlantic Ocean during the Second World War.
www.skylighters.org/special/queenmary/qmvoy4.html

ABOUT THE AUTHOR

Philomena Liggins is a trained designer and has worked in both education and industry. Since joining Bletchley Park as a Volunteer Tour Guide in 2007 she has developed an interest in war-time history, particularly the part that women played during both World Wars. She has written a number of articles and has given radio interviews on that subject. Her extensive research has enabled her to write the series of novels on the secret working of Bletchley Park's Government Code & Cypher School.

Together with her colleague, John Gallehawk, she is researching the development of the British Secret Service and their book, "Agents Aliens & Spies" will be published in the 2014.

HIDDEN TALENTS
PUBLISHING

Behind The Book

The Secret Lives at Bletchley Park Series

Moonlight Serenade – Secret Skies Over Bletchley Park

"Moonlight Serenade – Secret Skies Over Bletchley Park" is the second in the series and continues the story of code-breaking at Bletchley Park.

Six Rookie Wrens are drafted to F Block to work on German and Japanese codes. Initially shocked by the sheer size of the place and the seemingly mundane work they soon settle in with the help of their cigar smoking Chief Petty Officer.

Quartered together at Crawley Grange, a magnificent Tudor mansion, the girls are immediately captivated by its ghostly charm and waste little time in getting to know the young Allied aircrews training at RAF Cranfield and those stationed at the United States and British airfields near-by.

As the popular music of the American band leader Glenn Miller's "Moonlight Serenade" fills the air, love blossoms. Yet all too soon the secret world of Special Operations Executive and the dangerous moonlight missions undertaken by the pilots and crews of 138 and 161 Squadrons based at Tempsford make their mark.

Meanwhile back in Bletchley Park, with three of the girls operating the Tunny and Colossus machines, and the others working on calculations and Japanese ciphers, each one of them play their parts in decyphering those all important messages in the run up to the D-Day landings.

This is a story of love and romance highlighting the hidden fears and secrets of a group of young people working in that war-time station. Once again, in this place of contrasts, laughter and tears are mixed with the inevitable casualties of war; often where you least expect them.

Made in the USA
Lexington, KY
27 December 2015